REMBRANDT

LIFT PICTURE FOR TITLE AND COMMENTARY

REMBRANDT HARMENSZ VAN RIJN

REMBRANDT

TEXT BY

LUDWIG MÜNZ

Late Director, Akademische Gemäldegalerie, Vienna

WITH ADDITIONAL COMMENTARIES BY

BOB HAAK

Curator-in-Chief, Historical Museum, Amsterdam

———————

THE LIBRARY OF GREAT PAINTERS

HARRY N. ABRAMS, INC. *Publishers* NEW YORK

NOTE: The picture choice in this edition has been somewhat revised, since it has become possible to include works desired but unavailable when the book was originally published. The commentaries for the new color-plates are identified by the initials B. H.

REVISED EDITION

Standard Book Number 0-8109-0437-3
Library of Congress Catalog Card Number: 67–22766
HARRY N. ABRAMS, INCORPORATED, New York, N. Y.
Printed and bound in Japan.

CONTENTS

REMBRANDT HARMENSZ VAN RIJN by Ludwig Münz   7

ETCHINGS: *A Note and a Selection*   28

DRAWINGS: *A Note and a Selection*   42

COLORPLATES

SELF-PORTRAIT   *Kunsthistorisches Museum, Vienna*   *Frontispiece*

THE ANGEL AND THE PROPHET BALAAM   *Musée Cognacq-Jay, Paris*   59

SIMEON IN THE TEMPLE   *Kunsthalle, Hamburg*   61

SELF-PORTRAIT   *Mauritshuis, The Hague*   63

THE RAISING OF LAZARUS   *Collection Howard F. Ahmanson, Los Angeles*   65

SIMEON IN THE TEMPLE   *Mauritshuis, The Hague*   67

THE ANATOMY LESSON OF DR. TULP   *Mauritshuis, The Hague*   69

THE RAISING OF THE CROSS   *Pinakothek, Munich*   71

THE DESCENT FROM THE CROSS   *Pinakothek, Munich*   73

THE STORM ON THE SEA OF GALILEE   *Isabella Stewart Gardner Museum, Boston*   75

SAMSON THREATENING HIS FATHER-IN-LAW   *State Museums, Berlin-Dahlem*   77

THE BLINDING OF SAMSON   *Städelsches Kunstinstitut, Frankfurt*   79

DANAË   *The Hermitage, Leningrad*   81

THE ANGEL DEPARTING FROM THE FAMILY OF TOBIAS   *The Louvre, Paris*   83

LANDSCAPE WITH AN OBELISK   *Isabella Stewart Gardner Museum, Boston*   85

JOHN THE BAPTIST PREACHING   *State Museums, Berlin-Dahlem*   87

REMBRANDT'S MOTHER   *Kunsthistorisches Museum, Vienna*   89

REMBRANDT'S MOTHER (detail)   *Kunsthistorisches Museum, Vienna*   91

THE NIGHT WATCH (THE COMPANY OF CAPTAIN FRANS BANNING COCQ)
    Rijksmuseum, Amsterdam   93

THE NIGHT WATCH (detail)   *Rijksmuseum, Amsterdam*   95

THE HOLY FAMILY   *The Louvre, Paris*   97

THE WOMAN TAKEN IN ADULTERY   *National Gallery, London*   99

CHRIST AT EMMAUS   *The Louvre, Paris*   101

HANNAH AND SAMUEL   *Collection Earl of Ellesmere, London*   103

HEAD OF CHRIST   *State Museums, Berlin-Dahlem*   105

AN OLD MAN IN AN ARMCHAIR   *The Devonshire Collection, Chatsworth*   107

ARISTOTLE CONTEMPLATING THE BUST OF HOMER
  The Metropolitan Museum of Art, New York   109

BATHSHEBA   *The Louvre, Paris*   111

A WOMAN BATHING   *National Gallery, London*   113

JOSEPH ACCUSED BY POTIPHAR'S WIFE   *State Museums, Berlin-Dahlem*   115

JACOB BLESSING THE SONS OF JOSEPH   *Gemäldegalerie, Cassel*   117

JACOB BLESSING THE SONS OF JOSEPH (detail)   *Gemäldegalerie, Cassel*   119

SELF-PORTRAIT   *Kunsthistorisches Museum, Vienna*   121

TWO YOUNG NEGROES   *Mauritshuis, The Hague*   123

THE POLISH RIDER   *The Frick Collection, New York*   125

A BOY READING (TITUS)   *Kunsthistorisches Museum, Vienna*   127

MOSES BREAKING THE TABLETS OF THE LAW   *State Museums, Berlin-Dahlem*   129

ST. PETER DENYING HIS MASTER   *Rijksmuseum, Amsterdam*   131

JACOB WRESTLING WITH THE ANGEL   *State Museums, Berlin-Dahlem*   133

MATTHEW THE EVANGELIST   *The Louvre, Paris*   135

THE CIRCUMCISION   *The National Gallery of Art, Washington, D.C.*
  (Widener Collection)   137

THE SYNDICS (THE SAMPLING OFFICIALS OF THE DRAPERS' GUILD)
  Rijksmuseum, Amsterdam   139

THE CONSPIRACY OF THE BATAVIANS   *Nationalmuseum, Stockholm*   141

EQUESTRIAN PORTRAIT   *National Gallery, London*   143

THE BRIDAL COUPLE (THE JEWISH BRIDE)   *Rijksmuseum, Amsterdam*   145

A MARRIED COUPLE WITH THREE CHILDREN   *Herzog Anton-Ulrich Museum,*
  Brunswick   147

THE RETURN OF THE PRODIGAL SON   *The Hermitage, Leningrad*   149

SELF-PORTRAIT   *Mauritshuis, The Hague*   151

Rembrandt

ALTHOUGH the human feeling in Rembrandt's paintings is self-evident to everyone who has come under their spell, a short historical introduction may contribute to our understanding of this artist and his art. The political situation of Holland in his time, and more particularly the conditions that prevailed in his native town and his parental home, had a profound influence on his entire career.

In 1609, three years after Rembrandt's birth, the States General of the Netherlands concluded a hard-won truce with Spain, which secured Holland's religious and economic independence and created the necessary conditions for the flowering of her highly original art. For nearly half a century this little nation held the position of something like a great power, ruling the seas thanks to its victorious navy, and drawing rich profits from its colonial possessions. Only after 1650 was Holland obliged to relinquish her supremacy, little by little, to England and France.

In Rembrandt's lifetime Holland was a great mercantile power. Her middle-class urban civilization, partly founded on Calvinism, contrasted strikingly with that of the southern Lowlands—present-day Belgium—which had remained Catholic, and which continued for a long time to be part of the Hapsburg Empire. Life and culture in these southern provinces were influenced (as mainly in southern Europe, also) by the powerful secular rulers, the great princes of the Church, and the proud nobility. The situation was different in Holland, where a strongly united people had won their independence, were conscious of this achievement, and devoted themselves to peaceful and freedom-loving pursuits. Her citizens enjoyed a far greater degree of individual liberty than those of any other European nation. Like her sister-republic Venice, which also owed her greatness and independence to her position as a mercantile sea power, Holland produced an original kind of painting—somewhat akin, incidentally, to that of Venice. For various reasons—the impact of city life, the common prosperity that made life easier in these relatively small republics, and their numerous commercial contacts with other peoples—both Holland and Venice from the Renaissance on displayed in their art a particularly lively interest in the problems of giving form to the immediate natural and human environment.

There was, however, an essential difference between the two countries. In Venice, the aristocratic republic in the Catholic South, for all the joy evinced by its artists in rendering the world about them, its colorfulness, the *sfumato* of the damp sea air which softens hard outlines and mutes bright colors—a quality which Venice shares with Holland—the subject matter was predominantly religious and official: paintings served to decorate churches and to glorify the state, Venetian victories, and the power of the Doges. In Holland, the Calvinist republic in the North, the subject matter and the function of painting in the seventeenth century were quite different. Having destroyed the images in the churches, the Calvinists had no use for religious painting as ecclesiastical decoration. This is one reason why Dutch art differs so markedly from that of the southern Lowlands, from Rubens and his school, who produced large Baroque religious paintings and portraits of the famous and well born. In Holland, too, painters treated religious subjects, but such paintings were small and intended for moral edification; they served to decorate the walls of middle-class homes, or they were reproduced and circulated as engravings and etchings. The Dutch non-Catholic Christians—there were several sects, which lived essentially in harmony despite many theological quarrels—regarded themselves as a chosen people, particularly after their victory over Spain, and took it for granted that the examples of Biblical stories had a special relevance for them. However, the characteristic themes of their art were landscape and portrait.

Rembrandt belonged to the second generation of painters in free Holland. Those of the first generation had actually lived through the period of struggles before 1609 and had experienced the severe pressures to which their country had been subjected, as well as its final victory. They expressed their life and their newly won freedom in a self-assured, often presumptuous manner. Frans Hals, whose broadly painted portraits show burghers enjoying the present, may suffice as an example. At the same time, an original school of landscape painting had begun to develop. The second generation of Dutch painters, however, which included a number of important artists besides Rembrandt, were so sure of their freedom that they could turn to quite new and different problems.

Rembrandt was born in Leyden in 1606, the sixth child of a relatively prosperous miller. He attended the Latin school until 1620. By that time his gift for painting had been recognized. After a short apprenticeship in Leyden, and later in Amsterdam, under Lastman and Pynas, he worked independently from 1625 on in Leyden. In 1632 his reputation as a portraitist was so well established that the Surgeons' Guild of Amsterdam commissioned him to paint their group portrait, known as *The Anatomy Lesson of Dr. Tulp* (page 69). He moved to that city and remained there for the rest of his life.

In 1634 Rembrandt married Saskia van Uylenburgh, the orphaned daughter of a family much more prominent than his own. For the next ten years the successful portrait painter led a life of luxury and extravagance. He purchased a large house in the Jewish quarter on Joden-Breestraat, a street where many other artists lived; this step contributed to his later financial ruin. The end of the 1630s and the beginning of the 1640s were marked by events that deeply influenced his life. His mother, whom he had painted several times, died in 1640. In 1642 he lost his wife Saskia. Only one of their children, Titus, survived her. During that year he painted his large group portrait of the Company of Captain Frans Banning Cocq, the so-called *Night Watch* (page 93). Although he received other official commissions later, he spent the next ten years in semi-retirement, devoting himself solely to his work and surrounded by pupils and friends. His son Titus was under the charge first of Geertje Dircx, a trumpeter's widow, and then of Hendrickje Stoffels, who entered his home about 1645 while still a girl and remained his companion and faithful friend in all his troubles until her death.

In the early 1650s, just when Holland was entering upon a period of great crisis, the outward security of Rembrandt's existence was threatened by a disaster that he attributed to financial losses due to commercial enterprises. Overburdened with debts ever since the purchase of his house, he had to draw on the money from Saskia's estate that had been bequeathed to his son Titus. In 1656 he was obliged to declare himself insolvent, and in 1658 all of his possessions, including the house, were put up for auction. The results were altogether disappointing, and the prin-

1. JUDAS RETURNING THE THIRTY PIECES OF SILVER. 1629. Wood, 31 × 40¹/₂″. *Collection Marchioness of Normanby, London*

cipal creditors, excepting his son Titus, came out of it all but emptyhanded. Rembrandt moved to another neighborhood, Rozengracht. None of this crushed him as an artist, but he was obliged, in return for financial support, to hand over to Titus and Hendrickje any funds he realized from the sale of his works, and they, not he, were empowered to conclude contracts. Thus the last decade of his life, during which he created what are probably his greatest works, was marked by a new soberness. The legend that Rembrandt was utterly destitute and unrecognized at the time of his death has, however, been disproved by recent research. During this decade, at least at its beginning, he even obtained further official commissions. He was so famous that he also received orders for pictures from Italy *(Aristotle Contemplating the Bust of Homer*, page 109) and in 1667 a Medici prince called upon him. His misfortunes during this period were personal ones. In 1663 Hendrickje died. The year 1668 was a particularly unhappy one for

him; Titus married and only a short time later died, followed by his young wife. Rembrandt was left alone with his daughter Cornelia, whom Hendrickje had borne him. He died in October 1669, at the age of sixty-three.

Rembrandt's life was characteristic of an urban existence within a commercial, maritime nation like Holland. Passed within the narrow boundaries of his native land, it was marked only by such conflicts and troubles as may occur in the life of any man. What sets him apart as man and artist is the way in which the vicissitudes of his life failed to disturb his sense of his vocation. Despite his misfortunes, some of his own making, he remained unswervingly dedicated to his task as he saw it, proud to be a painter. As an artist he never surrendered; he made no compromises, even when by doing so he might have made his life easier. His artistic pride and devotion to his work are best illustrated by Baldinucci's statement that Rembrandt, when he was working, would refuse to receive any visitor, even a prince, rather than be disturbed. He was not a Renaissance artist like Leonardo and Titian, who needed music and conversation while they worked.

During the first half of the seventeenth century the painters of Europe, although they were divided into various schools, had one thing in common: all of them tried to produce an objective (that is, realistic) picture, without omitting any characteristic feature of the figures portrayed. These painters attempted to capture the colors of "reality" in the full range of tones, and light in all its variations. In a century dominated by the ideas of Galileo and Descartes, the painter's goal of producing the illusion of reality made new and different demands on him. This applies to artists of North and South alike, to Caravaggio and his followers in Italy, to Velázquez in Spain, and to the Le Nains or Georges de la Tour in France. It also applies to Rubens in Flanders, and even more to Frans Hals, and later to Rembrandt, Vermeer, and the great landscape painters of Holland.

The great, independent-minded Italian artist Michelangelo da Caravaggio (1573–1610) was the leading representative of this trend. He surpassed all earlier painters in his ability to give pictorial plasticity to his figures, modeling them sharply with light and shade so as to bring them out of the deepest shadow into the most brilliant light. Caravaggio exerted a fascination over the next generation of painters in both North and South; however, each artist interpreted him in his own way and produced paintings quite different from Caravaggio's. The formula for this way of seeing is visual realism: the portrayal of every detail of actuality. Nature alone must be the model; the grace, dignity, and decorum of Renaissance art no longer provided the standards. This was one of the basic tendencies of seventeenth-century art, however crucial the continuing influence of Raphael, Titian, and Michelangelo upon most painters. But it must be stressed that Caravaggio's realism was something beyond the mere depiction of dirty feet or the portrayal of only common people. Those who had not already known this realized it after the Caravaggio exhibition in Milan (1951), which revealed this great master's tragic, revolutionary art and at the same time the meaning of his realism.

At all events, Rembrandt impresses us from his earliest works as an arch-realist in the popular sense of the word, one who shocks the world and challenges it to contradict him. All that has come down to us of his youthful utterances points to his pride in his ability to portray the truth as he himself experienced it, without too great reliance upon teachers, solely from his own study of nature. That such was Rembrandt's attitude before 1630, when he worked in Leyden with another painter, Jan Lievens, we know from the account of Huygens, an erudite and prominent man, who was for a long time secretary to the Prince of Orange, Stadholder of the Netherlands. Huygens called on Rembrandt and Lievens, two young painters whose parents were of "lower-class" origin: Lievens' father was a dyer and Rembrandt's, as we know, a miller. Huygens said afterwards that both were bent upon achieving what they thought was true painting, devoting their full time to their work without regard for their health. When Huygens asked them why they did not go to Italy, where painters usually spent their years of apprenticeship, they answered—and it was characteristic of the Dutch of their time, of their burgher pride in their country's wealth and power—that they could see enough Italian pictures at home. The self-confidence of these young men of lowly origin, their very opportunity to follow the vocation of painter, was typical of this period of Dutch culture.

Thus, even in his early twenties, Rembrandt had achieved such reputation that men like Huygens came to visit him in Leyden, a city famous for its university founded to promote humanistic studies in contrast to the stress on theology elsewhere.

All this is essential for our understanding of Rembrandt and the works he produced while a young man. Where else but in the atmosphere of this university town could a young painter have produced *Judas Returning the Thirty Pieces of Silver* (figure 1) which Huygens mentioned as having moved him most profoundly? (Known from a number of copies for a long time, what seems to be the original of this painting has now been rediscovered.) This work shows us in a flash the kind of realism, the vision and experience of man, that Rembrandt wanted to express, and the use he made of light and shade, brightness and darkness, to create form. He went far beyond anything he could have learned from his teachers Lastman and Pynas, who had studied in Rome and assimilated the elements of Caravaggio's art. In this picture, the principal light glances off the books and the rabbi's table to fall on the thirty pieces of silver. Judas kneels in the foreground, half plunged in shadow. Only his face, distorted with anguish, and his wrung hands are in a glaring light; he is alone with his despair among the fat Pharisees and priests. These men, who led him into evil, are seated comfortably in the light with a greedy look in their eyes, or, as though they have forgotten that they themselves commissioned the treachery, are turning away in self-righteous pride from the despairing Judas. Light and shadow are not rigidly and academically subordinated to the linear composition of a triangle, at the apex of which the rabbi stands looking upon the scene with abhorrence; instead, they form a surprising contrast to the linear structure and compel us to direct our gaze where the painter, for all his realism, wants it directed—at the money, at the repentant Judas. Under the guise of a realistic rendering, a new possibility of artistic expression through contrast has been discovered. This painting affords us a haunting glimpse into the reality of that world which Rembrandt had from the outset striven to endow with form, to bring into the light.

Here, as subsequently throughout his life, Rembrandt's art—his paintings as well as his drawings and etchings—reveals the meaning of his realism, of what may seem at first glance a mere transcription of reality. Man is the sole object of his interest, and he studies and observes him as the vehicle of both good and evil. His painting reflects the knowledge that human beings—not excepting himself—are, for all their sinfulness, worthy objects of study and devotion. That Rembrandt chose such a subject as the penitence of Judas shows how far removed he was—as in all his works that illustrate the Old and New Testament—from traditional devotional painting; such a work as this one could never serve for an altarpiece. Judas, the most despised of men, remained for Rembrandt a human being worthy of our compassion because he repented.

Such a conception of Judas expresses a faith animated by inner freedom, and it suggests that Rembrandt's experience of the Scriptures enabled him as man and as artist to make independent decisions for which he alone felt responsible. Rembrandt was a Christian, although we do not know to what sect he officially belonged. In his works he defined, so to speak, his own position with regard to the controversies then dividing Holland's various Protestant denominations. Such controversies were frequently quite violent, despite the fact that Holland was tolerant and granted full citizenship to religious refugees from all over the world—the Hussites of Bohemia as well as the Jews of Portugal and Spain. One of the problems debated at the time was whether Christ, during His appearance on earth, had been God or man. Rembrandt, more than any other artist of the period, strove to give earthly reality to the face of Christ; and, at the same time, no one endowed that face with more radiant kindness—particularly in his later paintings. Such works, though radically different from so-called devotional pictures, reveal authentic religious feeling. Because of his profound experience of humanity, Rembrandt was able to portray man not only as sinful yet repentant (in his figure of

2. SASKIA VAN UYLENBURGH. 1641. Wood, $38^5/_8 \times 32^1/_4''$. *Gemäldegalerie, Dresden*

Judas), but also as a being of indescribable goodness and purity who sacrifices himself for mankind (in his figure of Christ).

When we speak of an artist and his work, we must throw as much light as possible on his basic motivations. That is why we have dwelt at some length on the *Judas* as an example illustrating Rembrandt's experience of man and his conception of humanity. Such an emphasis may seem excessive, for today Rembrandt's portraits, and his etchings and drawings that treat Christian subjects and the period when Christ walked on earth unrecognized, are chiefly appreciated for their "quiet inwardness." Like his admirers of earlier generations—Goethe, for instance—many of our contemporaries are so impressed by Rembrandt's modest serenity, or even by his naturalness and humility, that they generally forgive him his alleged inability to represent beauty, on the ground that he is realistic. Actually, Rembrandt's works reveal a new kind of beauty, far removed from the classical kind—a vision and an interpretation of man which transfigure the least beautiful face, the ugliest body.

3. Michelangelo da Caravaggio. THE CALLING OF ST. MATTHEW. 1597–98. *Church of San Luigi dei Francesi, Rome*

Rembrandt may seem to have departed completely from the artistic conventions of his time, but in fact he exploited them for his own purposes, and we can understand his works only if we take the time to study them at length. Only then do we discover, in such a painting as the *Judas*, the richness of the light in the chiaroscuros and indirect reflections. We gradually realize that such naturalistic pictures have a deeper meaning, and that Rembrandt, who had completely mastered all the laws of logical linear composition developed by the Renaissance (for example, the triangular structure), was at the same time moved by profound feeling, and in portraying faces was more concerned with the expression of spirituality than with the external features.

Such expressive values stand out more clearly in the sketchy early etchings than in the paintings, where they are to some extent concealed by the vivacity and the polyphonic orchestration of the color. If we look at Rembrandt's self-portrait of 1629 (figure 25), we note that an expression of anger has been achieved in this etching through non-naturalistic, expressive line, such as the zigzag of the eyebrows. The anger is communicated to us because the line records it in terms of our own muscular reactions. Such emotionally determined draftsmanship achieves a semblance of reality that a photograph could never give. In other words, although the effect of the work is realistic, it is achieved by expressive means that have nothing in common

with merely imitative, superficial renderings of reality.

We find the same directness of expression, this time in the primitive emotion of awe before a miracle, as in *The Raising of Lazarus* (page 65). The figure of Christ, which at first glance seems to be of natural size, is upon closer examination discovered to be gigantic in relation to the figure of the resurrected man. The effect is the same as that of medieval miniatures, in which the supernatural power of Christ is suggested by a figure of superhuman dimensions, without regard for the coherence of spatial relationships. The supernatural quality of the miracle-worker in Rembrandt's picture is just as convincing, and it is conveyed more subtly because his Christ is integrated within a space that is rendered realistically by means of light, shade, and color. To paint, draw, or etch like this requires a special courage—an inner freedom unconcerned with tidy execution—which communicates the experience uncompromisingly by means of expressive signs through lines, chiaroscuro, and color.

Another self-portrait, painted probably two years earlier, is characteristic of Rembrandt's youthful work when he was so violently attracted to the extreme possibilities of experience. In this, Rembrandt painted himself standing half in shadow, as though playing the part of the unobserved observer. By his rapid, sketchlike technique—he used the wooden tip of his brush to scratch out the hair—Rembrandt achieves in this picture an effect of the casually glimpsed, and at the same time one of defiant, uncompromising vision. Here the artist is a curious yet calmly detached observer recording an event—a physically unattractive man, who nonetheless comes very close to us with his vision, with all his strength and weakness. We understand why Rembrandt considered the physical and spiritual representation of man to be the most serious and significant task for a painter.

This technique of quick, incisive line—as in the example of drawing the hair with the brush-handle, providing high lights at the same time—was not accidental in Rembrandt's work, nor confined to small sketches such as the self-portrait. The same technique was employed in the fully finished early paintings. The paintings dating from 1626 onward have in common a vivid palette, with further accentuation in the application of local color, and a sharp chiaroscuro that goes back to Caravaggio. The technique of blending the various color tones of a face and of making them merge into one another so as to accentuate texture and relief was also derived from Caravaggio. But Rembrandt departed from Caravaggio's static style, and his unconventionality and originality are present even in these early works. Besides his use of the wooden tip of his brush to scratch out high lights in the hair, there are the rapid, vigorous rhythms of his brushwork which give liveliness to the painting, and there is his practice of scattering isolated spots of strong color at various unexpected places to vary and enliven the otherwise too smooth and static composition. To Rembrandt, every single color had from the outset greater expressive power than it had ever had before. In this respect he differs fundamentally from the Dutch painters of his youth, and from Vermeer a little after him, whose work is characterized by a quiet, still-life quality that recalls Caravaggio's early style.

Discussion of Rembrandt always puts more emphasis on his use of shadow than his use of light; we are told that his figures stand out in relief from the darkness, or that they are absorbed within it. For this reason it is important to note that seldom in his career did Rembrandt employ the red or dark brown bolus ground (priming) of the Italians, so characteristic of southern Baroque with its clearly articulated divisions between light and shade. Like his Dutch contemporaries, Rembrandt utilized a brighter underpainting which enabled him, for instance, to obtain effects of subdued lighting when he scratched through to it. The background pillars in *Simeon in the Temple* (page 61) at The Hague derive their brilliance from the fact that the darker, gray-green overpainting has been partly scratched away. This produces a more evanescent and yet more brilliant tone than would be obtained by laying the color on directly. The subdued brightness guides the eye to the center of the picture, as though accidentally, because the main group is placed just in front of the luminous pillar. Thus we see how Rembrandt, to a much greater extent than any painter before him, assigned to light and color a function that usually appears to be performed by the linear composition alone: the function of an expressive medium. He accomplishes this in a very plausible and unobtrusive manner, so that the effect is achieved slowly and imperceptibly. Rembrandt discovered these potentialities of artistic expression and this orchestration of their effects entirely independently.

Rembrandt began as a painter with studies in expression like the small self-portrait mentioned above, with individual heads, and small-sized historical compositions. Not until 1630 did he begin to paint portraits in the manner that was to bring him fame and reputation during the next ten years. In his youth he was attracted primarily by Biblical stories, which he painted as though they were actually taking place before him. In his earliest period, he painted such scenes in a vigorous manner, modeling the relatively large figures in the small paintings with strong cast shadows. After 1628, the figures remain frontal, but the scene is viewed from an unexpected angle. From the outset he had demonstrated an impressive capacity for sharp characterization by means of light and color. But as early as 1628 or 1629, while he was still in Leyden, he revealed another new potentiality of artistic expression. From now on Rembrandt's effort to represent man in his physical reality, with all his faults and passions, emphasizes man in his relation to his environment and to space. During this period he is concerned, even more than with the individual figures themselves, with the way they move in the chiaroscuro of space, in all their smallness, in their natural scale. There develops that series of paintings which, for all their colorfulness—his quiet way of handling space is repeatedly interrupted by strong color contrasts—are justly considered examples of the style known as *Tonmalerei*. This we may render as "tonal painting"—that is, painting in harmonious, restrained tones closely related in value. A gamut of broken colors, which merge into one another from gray to green to brown, produces the illusion of continuous space as we experience it.

Rembrandt was not the first to represent three-dimensional space in this way. The Dutch landscape painters whose pictures were based on their observation of the vast plains and the sky—from Esaias van de Velde to Jan van Goyen—were precursors of Rembrandt's tonal painting. It was Rembrandt, however, who utilized this style to introduce a new aspect of realism—the interdependence of all external events in space. While thus solving another artistic problem, he mastered one more potentiality of expression unknown to his predecessors. He could now give his figures depth and at the same time show them surrounded by air, without isolating them; the works of other painters, in comparison, often seem flat and two-dimensional. Whereas a *Descent from the Cross* by Rubens (figure 4) seems like a wonderfully colored relief, the same scene by Rembrandt (page 73), arranged diagonally against the evening light, is endowed with life; the viewer is made part of the picture, so to speak. Another of Rembrandt's artistic devices was to place large figures close to us in the foreground; we see them as if we were standing quite near them. By this means the momentary, contingent character of the action is brought out—since we ourselves are witnessing it. Making use of the current national style of tonal painting, and destroying it in the process, Rembrandt achieved a new means of rich, polyphonic expressiveness.

Whereas other painters confined themselves to a narrow range of tones, low-keyed in value, Rembrandt interposed stronger tones wherever he thought

4. Peter Paul Rubens. THE DESCENT FROM THE CROSS. 1613.
Wood, 165¼ × 122″. *Cathedral, Antwerp*

kerchief over her head, she looks at us out of red-rimmed eyes. How else could Rembrandt have given us, not only pleasure in his mother's lovely costume, but an impression of the ravages of time, and how else could he have graduated his tones, had he not placed the glowing gold of her jewelry almost in the center of the painting? Only thus could he create his magnificent portrait of a true matriarch—*naer het leven*—with his mother's face for model.

Of course, to the academically trained artist, as to many of Rembrandt's earliest biographers, a painter who would carry his search for truth so far as to make changes in his pictures up to the very last moment, scarcely troubling to conceal earlier stages, must seem eccentric. Rembrandt's practice is accounted for by the fact that he was driven, obsessed by the idea that his final version must also be the truest. Time and again he made changes even in finished works, but he always did this with great mastery. For instance, in many of Rembrandt's etchings we are not at first glance aware of any such changes until we scrutinize them in detail; only then do we realize that earlier states are still visible under the vigorous correction of a few lines. Of course, today we enjoy participating in the creation of a work of art—it is an element of contemporary taste—and recognizable corrections of this kind give added charm. Similarly, we take special pleasure in Rembrandt's powerful brush strokes, the vividness and individuality of which are more visible today than in Rembrandt's own lifetime, because the varnish has darkened in the depressions and accentuated the relief of the painted surface.

As we look at Rembrandt's works we should never forget that for all his breadth of experience and the extent of his creative activity, marked by many artistic discoveries, his basic impulse remained the same throughout his career. We have anticipated Rembrandt's development in order to illustrate the use he made of the seemingly picturesque and the bizarre, as for instance in his relating of bright lighting and bright tones to shadow. However, in order to explain how such technical means were used by him to achieve tragic tension in works that appear, at first sight, quite unassuming and conventional, we must return to our chronological examination of the works he produced in the 1630s.

The field of painting in which Rembrandt achieved popularity from 1630 on was that of representing the human figure, most often in life-size, half-length portraits. At that time portrait painting was in its heyday in Holland. Besides Frans Hals there were a number of successful portraitists of the older generation such as Mierevelt, Elias, and De Keyser, but they confined themselves in their straightforward portraits

this necessary. His practice in this respect is one reason why critics and connoisseurs of his own day did not understand him, and described him as a bizarre painter giving way to any passing mood. Thus, Houbraken relates that in one work, in order to enhance the brilliant luminosity of a pearl, he painted over the rest of the picture to make it dimmer—thus ruining, according to the story, a painting which represented Cleopatra. Such a judgment would be correct in the case of ordinary Baroque paintings, but in Rembrandt's case the procedure was quite natural. It is by such devices that he makes us experience so many different, previously unexplored possibilities through his almost awe-inspiring vision of men and situations. For instance, in the marvelous portrait of his mother (pages 89 and 91), of 1639, the year before she died, the jewelry on her bosom is in brighter light than her wrinkled face. Half enveloped in the shadow of the to a limited range of impressionistic effects. The works of these artists served Rembrandt in his early period as models for his own much more vivid portraits.

In the field of representational painting Holland introduced a new pictorial genre, distinct both from religious painting and from the historical painting of Catholic countries: the large group portrait, picturing corporations such as those of the surgeons, guardsmen, or drapers. These corporations frequently had the character of benevolent as well as professional associations. Although he shared his basic conception of the group portrait with other artists, Rembrandt from the very outset solved its problems in his own way. Where the others invariably show the human figure at rest, producing a character study with each subject set advantageously in bright light, Rembrandt endows his portraits with a fresh, original, and surprisingly authentic animation.

We have mentioned Rembrandt's great gift for expressive characterization, as manifested in his Biblical scenes and his sketches. His portrait technique is essentially the same. His portraits owe their vitality to the fact that in them the excessive sharpness of his linear characterization in the various parts of the face has been brought together into over-all unity by means of coloring, lighting, and shading. To Rembrandt each part of the face, the individual eye, every single feature, has its own expressively vigorous life. Each hand is endowed with its own special power of expression. Rembrandt transformed the stolidity of the Dutch into activity or, at least, into a transient mood. The human beings he painted seem to breathe within three-dimensional space—that is to say, the background is no longer merely a painted surface, but is full of mysterious animation. Its colorfulness, the variation of the tones, produce a depth and a vibration in the air, a *sfumato* out of which the portrait figure emerges in the round, and yet at the same time remains inseparable from its environment, thanks to Rembrandt's own kind of chiaroscuro, the darkness of space. It might seem, in view of the simplicity of Dutch costume in the period, and in view of the style, current in the 'thirties, of placing the portrait figure against a vaporous gray background, that the artist had little room for variation. Rembrandt, however, that unique dramatist among Dutch painters, succeeded in producing portraits full of tension and inner movement.

It was for his portraiture, not for his Biblical scenes, that he was called to Amsterdam, where he lived from 1631 on. The commission he received was of a kind possible at that time only in Holland. The Governors of the Surgeons' Guild, headed by Dr. Nicolaes Tulp, wished to be immortalized in a portrait; and Rembrandt, whose reputation was founded on single portraits, was invited to Amsterdam. *The Anatomy Lesson of Dr. Tulp* (page 69) opens the series of Rembrandt's portraits of burghers; for more than a decade he was kept very busy executing their commissions. Even this first *Anatomy Lesson* is a work full of revolutionary tensions. What is so epoch-making, so crucial about this painting, and what distinguishes it from previous treatments of similar subjects is, first of all, the conception of space and of the action portrayed.

In earlier paintings, such as Mierevelt's *Anatomy* (figure 6), which served as model for the composition, or in other works of this kind, the corpse had been treated merely as the emblem of the Surgeons' Guild, and, for all the realism of the treatment, was represented as quite small in relation to the figures of the surgeons. In Rembrandt's painting the corpse was given entirely new meaning by the composition and the arrangement of light and color. Here, because the light falls on it, the body becomes one of the focal centers of our interest. The rigid, dissected cadaver lies gray and yellow in full light. The figures of the surgeons are grouped to the left; they are subordinated to the corpse which provides the subject matter of the lesson, and to the teacher who is explaining the structure of the arm muscles, as he lays them bare with his scalpel. Dr. Tulp is seated a little to the right, behind the body, forming the apex of a triangular composition. Thus an element of tension has been introduced into a kind of painting that hitherto had represented all figures as of equal importance. Here the teacher is emphasized by his place apart. It is, however, from the contrasts between the linear composition and the interplay of colors that the real life of this painting derives. It is characteristic of Rembrandt's genius in handling color and light that this emphasized figure seems to occupy a natural place in the composition, a place that is taken for granted. The resulting effect of reality and dramatic tension nearly removes the painting from the category of portraiture, ordinarily expressive of uniform calm. The physician, a man whose knowledge and skill make him in Rembrandt's eyes a true servant of the people, has been placed in the center next to the dead body, while the other figures, to whom the physician is lecturing, have been pushed to the side. By means of the diagonal position of the corpse and the Baroque lighting, the arrangement of the figures appears very natural. What might have been a conventional group portrait has acquired a new and deeper meaning that reflects Rembrandt's conception of the physician.

We have emphasized this painting as an example of Rembrandt's work in the period of his early success, because the manner in which it solved certain problems forecasts another work: *The Night Watch* (pages

93 and 95), painted ten years later, which became one of Rembrandt's most controversial works, and in which he solved an artistically related problem. The men whose portraits Rembrandt painted in *The Anatomy Lesson* did not at first realize that his purpose was not to flatter their vanity, but to portray their human qualities. In it, he had sought to bring out that aspect of a doctor's or an anatomist's activity which is of more than limited, temporal significance, by creating the image of a physician who serves mankind and teaches others how to serve. This image impresses us all the more deeply because the painting seems at first nothing more than a realistic rendering of a lecture, contrasting the calm, deliberate teacher with the stark cadaver.

More than two-thirds of Rembrandt's portraits of burghers date from the 'thirties. It was during that decade that he also produced other paintings, and above all drawings and etchings that were apparently closer to his heart; these works embody a profound conception of humanity, and they are as alive today as when they were created. It was typical of Rembrandt that when, in 1632, he was commissioned by the Stadholder to paint a series illustrating the Passion, he began with *The Raising of the Cross* (page 71) and *The Descent from the Cross*—in painting these scenes he could draw upon previous experience—and did not paint the opening scenes of the series, *The Birth of Christ* and *The Circumcision*, until the 'forties. His study of the cadaver preparatory to *The Anatomy Lesson*, also painted in 1632, doubtless influenced his rendering of the body of Christ in *The Descent from the Cross* (page 73).

This work is an impressively realistic representation of Christ's passion, of His sacrifice, and of the end of His earthly existence; nothing in it recalls the decorative character of traditional religious painting. Equally significant is the fact that in these paintings Rembrandt portrays himself almost obtrusively; hardly any painter before him had done this. In *The Raising of the Cross*

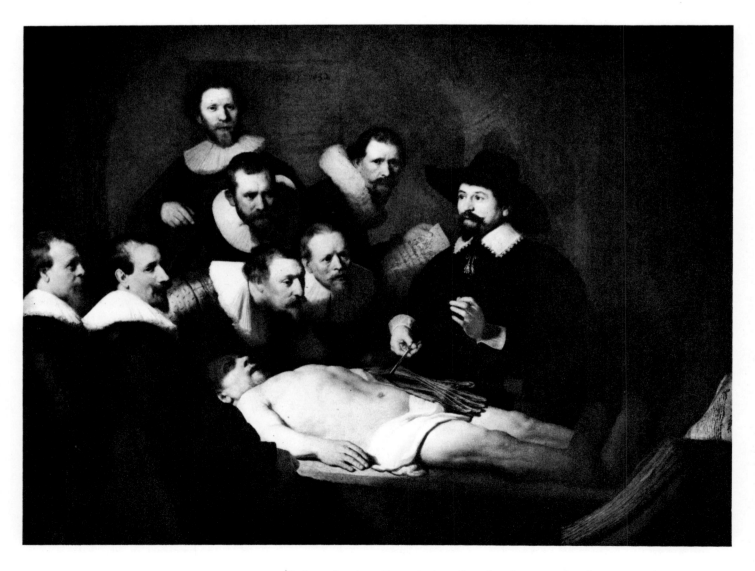

5. THE ANATOMY LESSON OF DR. TULP (before cleaning. For painting after cleaning see colorplate, page 69)

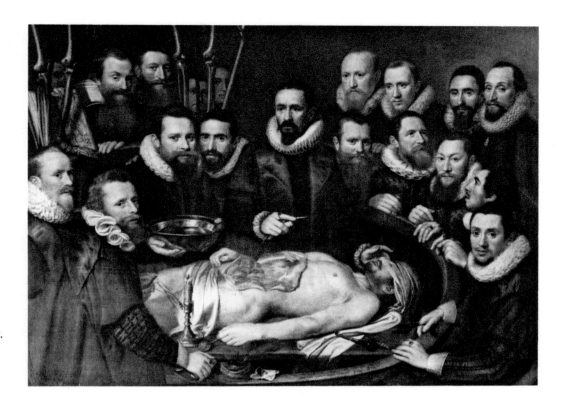

6. Michiel Janszen Mierevelt.
THE ANATOMY LESSON OF
DR. VAN DER NEER. 1617.
Hospital, Delft

Rembrandt is one of the soldiers (figure 10). In *The Descent from the Cross* he is the mourning figure in blue, penitent and shaken with suffering, who helps remove Christ's body. The desire to portray himself sharing in the suffering and the guilt was so important to Rembrandt that in an etching reproducing *The Descent from the Cross*, his face, expressing pain and compassion, is executed even more clearly than in the painting, where it is only dimly recognizable in the deep shadow.

During those years he painted *The Good Samaritan* —the stranger who gives help while a fellow countryman passes by indifferent to suffering; *The Return of the Prodigal Son* (page 149); *Christ Presented to the People;* and a number of other works dealing with relations between men and women, with sensuality, love, compassion, and betrayal. It may appear surprising, but it is characteristic of Rembrandt that during the happiest and most prosperous years of his life—he had married in 1634—his incorruptible vision seized upon such subjects and gave them form. The so-called self-portrait in Dresden, with Saskia on his knees, has long been recognized as an illustration for the Biblical story of the prodigal son.

In the very large *Blinding of Samson* (page 79), dated 1636, the extreme horror and brutality of this scene of betrayal and mutilation are depicted in striking color. It was followed in 1639 by the painting in which we see Delilah making her fatal decision, and by an etching of Adam and Eve, of unsurpassable realism. The painting of the myth of *Danae* (page 81) dates from

1636, *Susanna at the Bath* from 1637. From about the same time, also, is one of his most famous paintings (page 87), the monochrome *John the Baptist Preaching*, a composition which later, in the 'fifties, Rembrandt was to enlarge and alter considerably. Rembrandt could paint most effectively only that which he had intimately experienced, and it is as though with his marriage he had discovered a new world of passion governed by immutable laws, which he felt impelled to render with the utmost realism in a succession of works embodying new solutions of artistic problems.

Although Rembrandt's development is foreshadowed in his works of the 'thirties, he attained full mastery only in the beginning of the 'forties, with *The Night Watch*, his largest extant work (page 93). The artistic problem Rembrandt had to solve in this second of his group portraits, representing the Company of Captain Banning Cocq, was essentially the same as that of *The Anatomy Lesson*. He wanted to go beyond the conventional group portrait showing a number of individuals as they appear in real life, in order to produce a work full of dramatic tension.

Rembrandt, the artist, utilized the occasion to create a work of impressive power, illustrating the way people fall into a procession under the leadership of the man who guides them. Instead of a tranquil, static group portrait, he painted a mighty masterpiece, which inevitably raised a number of problems quite apart from the fact that his sitters felt slighted. In this work he expended his great artistic powers on an ephemeral event, really a subject for genre painting. This episode

17

7. Page from the family album of Capt. Frans Banning Cocq, showing a watercolor drawing by an anonymous contemporary artist of THE NIGHT WATCH in its original composition. *Exhibited at the Rijksmuseum, Amsterdam*

was a parade march; the painting is called *The Night Watch* only because the accumulated layers of yellow varnish gradually darkened and, before the recent cleaning, gave a night atmosphere to a march that actually had been represented as taking place in the light of late afternoon. Rembrandt made of this group portrait a work full of elemental human power, which transcends the historical significance of the subject, despite the costume pageantry that he still tended to overemphasize at this period. Out of the chaos of the background, with its contrasting tones and lines, an authentic order arises, as the captain—the only figure dressed in dark clothes, and surrounded by the brightest colors—points the way and carries the others along with him in a vigorous forward movement. Here colors attain their full expressive power, both illumi-

nating and stridently contrasting with each other. In Rembrandt's previous paintings, for all the vigor of the colors, the chiaroscuro had seemed to dominate.

The Night Watch with its ostentatious use of color still falls within Rembrandt's prosperous period. From the same period we have an etched *Self-Portrait* freely based on a painting by Raphael. This work, dating from 1639, was not unjustly chosen as the model of the boastful pseudo-Bohemian self-portraits of artists of the Victorian era. How much purer, and how far removed from the bravado necessary to the solution of such a problem as that presented by *The Night Watch*, is the effect of *The Sacrifice of Manoah* (figure 13). The first version of this subject dates from the same time, and in it Rembrandt used vigorous, luminous colors to a far greater extent than he had in previous paintings.

Such emotionally modulated colors reveal Rembrandt's mature understanding of colors, of their warmth and of their psychological interrelationships.

And yet *The Night Watch*, for all its artistic limitations, forced him as almost no other of his works did to revise and renew his whole painting technique. If color contrasts were to be effective in a painting of such enormous size, means other than those in earlier works on a smaller scale had to be employed. Nevertheless, Rembrandt's use of color in this work is essentially an extension of the procedures he employed earlier.

In the latter, he had developed a quality of coloristic effects similar to those produced by his expressive pen or by his strongly contrasted brush strokes; but the contrasts seem less "open" because they are subordinated to the over-all coherence of the subdued harmonies of tonal painting. Because of its large size, *The Night Watch* demanded an extension of the lesson which years of experience had taught, namely, that effects of color as well as effects of chiaroscuro may be obtained by contrasts which combine to form the picture in the eye of the beholder only from a given distance. In his effort to master an enormous surface, Rembrandt employed every device he had tried out in earlier works. Where previously his technique had blended colors to endow his figures with plasticity in the Caravaggesque

9. CHRIST BEFORE PILATE (large plate). 1635. Etching (state III), $21^5/_8 \times 17^1/_2$". *The Pierpont Morgan Library, New York*

8. THE ANGEL APPEARING TO THE SHEPHERDS. 1634. Etching (state III), $10^1/_4 \times 8^5/_8$". *The Pierpont Morgan Library, New York*

sense, now he achieved related but stronger effects by building up his picture, wherever necessary, with thick lumps of pigment, almost modeling it. At the same time he now juxtaposed colors with broad brush strokes, each separate, each vigorously and distinctly different, with the result that the colors combine into a living picture only when seen from a distance. The beholder must let the painting create itself all over again before him each time he looks at it; seen at close quarters, it is nothing but an aggregate of disconnected spots of color and strongly modeled details. This change of technique, which implies a change of experience, rids Rembrandt's painting of its last links with the static painting in local color of earlier periods, and produces a hauntingly realistic effect while enhancing the emotional force of the color tones.

This kind of painting, which gives us vibrating life instead of rigid representation, has its precedents, like other kinds of painting. In the deeper sense, it derives from the works painted in his old age by Titian, who was followed by such other Venetian painters as Tintoretto and the Bassani. But Rembrandt differs from these by his use of their "impressionistic" pictorial means. What narrow-minded, pedantic critics of his

10. SELF-PORTRAIT. Detail of THE RAISING OF THE CROSS.
1632–33. *Pinakothek, Munich*

own and later times condemned as error or limitation was actually the basic condition of his art, and that which accounts for its superiority. Concerning the paintings of the early period we have Rembrandt's own instructions, given on the occasion of delivering a picture from the Passion cycle: "You must hang my paintings in the brightest light." He demanded this in order to force the viewer to look at the painting the right way, to enable him to see the rich gradations of light and shadow, each degree of which has a significance of its own. Rembrandt's later technique, which makes the picture come into being and pass away, as it were, before the beholder, achieves a new and living intensity that did not exist in earlier painting, not even in that of Titian. Anyone wishing to experience these paintings will discover that his own motion, as he walks back and forth until he finally sees the picture, actually establishes the subjective condition for his insight. Even in the France of Louis XIV, where Rembrandt's art met with resistance, this fact was recognized by enlightened connoisseurs and by classicist theoreticians like Félibien.

As in the case of the youthful works, we gain closer insight into the spirit of these paintings when we attempt to understand the technique employed—in itself seemingly arbitrary and chaotic, and yet to Rembrandt the means with which he expressed the full range of human feeling in all its warmth, as only he could do.

11. THE GOOD SAMARITAN. 1633. Etching (state IV),
$10^1/_8 \times 8^5/_8$". *The Pierpont Morgan Library, New York*

12. Drawing after Raphael's PORTRAIT OF CASTIGLIONE.
Pen and wash, $6^3/_8 \times 8^1/_8$". *Albertina, Vienna*

13. THE SACRIFICE OF MANOAH. 1641 (with later corrections). Canvas, 95 ¹/₄ × 111 ³/₈″. *Gemäldegalerie, Dresden*

Rembrandt's technique involved the simultaneous use of pictorial means that would seem mutually exclusive not only in his own time, but even more so in the art of modern times. In Rembrandt's works after 1640 we note, adjacent to the dynamic brush strokes, isolated spots of various colors equal in size, laid on quietly but firmly at various places in the painting. In addition to the brush with which he painted one transparent layer of paint over another, covering it with glazes, he used his palette knife to lay on thick masses of pigment, or, where the effect requires it, to scratch off the paint and thus expose portions of the brighter underpainting—as he had done in his youth with the wooden tip of his brush. Only by these varied and different technical means do the paintings achieve their deeply moving and subtly nuanced effects. The techniques of our modern painters, or, more accurately, of the ances-

tors of modern painting, are fundamentally different because they stress only one mode of expression exploiting it exclusively. Rembrandt attempted to master more and different possibilities of expression than, say, Van Gogh or Cézanne. In Van Gogh's painting everything is concentrated in the expressiveness of broad strokes of the brush or palette knife, heavy with impasto, and in his eloquent curved lines. No element in the painting escapes the overemphasis on expressiveness. In Rembrandt's paintings portions have been laid on even more thickly than in Van Gogh's, with a broader brush or with the palette knife, but the fundamental difference is that in addition to conveying a *furioso* of experience in the leaping, flaming brush strokes, Rembrandt could also achieve in the same painting deep, luminous color effects by means of color harmonies and the application of several glazes.

14. Detail of THE NIGHT WATCH (see colorplate, page 93)

In order to clarify the similarities and the differences between Rembrandt and Cézanne, we quote here the following description by Baldinucci of Rembrandt's working methods, based on statements by the painter Keil, who was Rembrandt's pupil for eight years:

"This painter, different in his mental make-up from other people as regards self-control, was also most extravagant in his style of painting and evolved for himself a manner which may be called entirely his own, that is, without contour or limitation by means of inner and outer lines, but entirely consisting of violent and repeated strokes, with great strength of darks after his own fashion, but without any profound darks. And that which is almost impossible to understand is this: how, painting by means of these strokes, he worked so slowly, and completed his things with a tardiness and toil never equalled by anybody. He could have painted a great number of portraits, owing to the great prestige which in those parts had been gained by his coloring, to which his drawing did not, however, come up; but after it had become commonly known that whoever wanted to be portrayed by him had to sit to him for some two or three months, there were few who came forward. The cause of his slowness was that, immediately after the first work had dried, he took it up again, repainting it with bigger or smaller strokes, so that at times the pigment in a given place was raised more than half the thickness of a finger. Hence it may be said of him that he always toiled without rest, painted much, and completed very few pictures. Nevertheless, he always managed to retain such an esteem that a drawing by him, in which little or nothing could be seen, was sold by auction for 30 scudi, as is told by Bernardo Keillh of Denmark, the much-praised painter now working in Rome. This extravagance of manner was entirely consistent with Rembrandt's mode of living, since he was a most temperamental man and despised everyone. The ugly and plebeian face by which he was ill-favored was accompanied by untidy and dirty clothes, since it was his custom, when working, to wipe his brushes on himself, and to do other things of a similar nature. When he worked he would not have granted an audience to the first monarch in the world, who would have had to return and return again until he had found him no longer engaged upon that work."[1]

This description shows that in his later years, after about 1650, Rembrandt worked very slowly, setting down one spot of color next to another with great deliberation. This method is somewhat related to Cézanne's. Furthermore, like the aged Rembrandt, Cézanne wanted his sitters to be available over long periods of time. Both artists were interested in something other than producing likenesses; for both, the important thing was to achieve the particular impression they had in mind. They differ only in that Cézanne created a silent, haunting, spatial configuration with bright colors, piecing together a calm, classical picture out of parts of equal value; whereas the older Rembrandt grew, the more firmly he pursued the goal of giving form to his own experience through developing an individual color technique. Even though Rembrandt set one spot of color down carefully next to another spot of color, his technique was far more complex than Cézanne's, and his purpose basically different. However serene Rembrandt's painting may seem at first glance, his aim was to express the inexhaustible plenitude of life. His manner of contrasting chiaroscuros and luminous colors with broken ones creates new and unexpected expressive possibilities, which lead away from, not toward, repose. Anyone who can experience colors as fully as a musician can experience tones, harmonies, and dissonances, knows how much more intensely colors glow when they are put on as isolated spots of solid pigment—as are those little patches of the strongest yellow or blue in Rembrandt's pictures. Likewise, the effect of his broken colors and of his glazes, particularly when he chose for the uppermost surface a darker, almost dirty glaze of broken color, is much more striking: he can produce a mysterious luminous glow in those colors, as for instance in his frequent deep reds.

In the 'forties, however, Rembrandt did not achieve with this technique the epoch-making masterpieces that he created later. During this decade, withdrawing into himself because of his misfortunes, he produced his most intimate paintings. For all their dramatic tension—always present in a work by Rembrandt—the paintings of this period are the most optimistic in outlook. He tried to rediscover the ideals of his youth,

after the turmoil of the 'thirties when he had been so happy, so extravagant, and so brilliant. Now Rembrandt, for whom, characteristically, man and the rendering of human experience were so important, turned to landscapes and was far more attracted by nature's freedom than ever before, and not only by scenes full of pathos and wild agitation such as he had painted earlier. *The Three Trees* (figure 31) and other landscapes date from this time. Rembrandt leaves the active world of *The Night Watch*, where everything— light and shade and color—served the purpose of bringing the figure of the marching captain forward into the light.

The etching *Christ Healing the Sick* (figure 32; called "The Hundred Guilder Print" because of the high price it fetched even in Rembrandt's day) is perhaps one of the turning points in this process of self-rediscovery. It is a work that only Rembrandt could

15. Studies for JOHN THE BAPTIST PREACHING (see colorplate, page 87). About 1637. Pen and bistre, 6⁵/₈ × 7³/₄″. *Print Room, Berlin*

16. Sketch of frame for JOHN THE BAPTIST PREACHING. About 1650. Pen and wash, 5⁷/₈ × 8″. *The Louvre, Paris*

[1] From Filippo Baldinucci, *Cominciamento e progresso dell'arte d'intagliare in rame colla vita de' più eccelenti maestri della stessa professione*, Florence, 1686, translated by Tancred Borenius in *Rembrandt*, London, Phaidon Press, 1942.

23

have executed in chiaroscuro. In this print every conceivable relationship among men—the full range of their pride, doubt, and need—comes to life within the same space and under the same lighting. The light is so distributed that each figure receives the precise amount of brightness it requires. At the point of greatest brilliance, the scribe's expression of doubt is dissolved. The host of the sick move through every degree of light and shade and back again, in this mild light which gradually discloses a central focus, to which everything is subordinated and toward which everything moves—the Mediator, to whom the innocent child is closer than all adult wisdom.

Those years when Rembrandt's son Titus was a child are years of quiet concentration far from ordinary social activity. The paintings done in that period are often quite small. Rembrandt's new approach to artistic problems reflects his relations with his closest intimates, including Jews, whose faith in the coming of a Messiah and in the redemption of the world he had probably already known during his years of opulence when he had lived with Saskia in the house in the Jewish quarter. Rembrandt never portrayed the Redeemer so humble and humane for all His exalted stature, as in *Christ at Emmaus* (page 101), now in the Louvre. Here he gave Christ the features of a Jew— which is historically correct and in accordance with the Gospels—and probably used his friend, the Jewish physician Ephraim Bonus, as his model (figure 33). He saw in the face of a modest servant of mankind that goodness and faith in heavenly grace that had for him become reality in Christ.

There are several reasons why Rembrandt's late works, which so often strike us as more moving than his early ones, did not bring him in his own lifetime the success he expected. In the first place, Holland began at that time to lose her position of supremacy. Second, as early as 1650, there occurred a far-reaching shift in Dutch taste, bringing it closer to the French. All the Dutch painters whom we today consider the greatest, including Rembrandt and later Ruisdael, were affected by this crisis. The well-fed burghers could no longer follow their artists where the latters' very freedom led them. All the artists who refused to bow to the new French fashion were similarly treated. In addition, there is crucial significance in the fact that Rembrandt's defiant attitude provoked hostility. Heedless of external adversity, he had from the 'forties on withdrawn from social life to concentrate exclusively on his work. The recorded statements attributed to him may actually be his—not only those relating to technique, as when he said: "The paint smells bad, move farther back," or "I am a painter, not a dyer," but also that remark which has been so overworked:

"A painting is finished when the artist has achieved his purpose." We witness once again the tragic struggle between the artist aware of the revolutionary significance of his work, and the beholder who judges it presumptuously and hurriedly.

Rembrandt's most mature works date from the last two decades of his life. The loss of his money, his collection of art treasures, and (in 1658) his luxurious home on Joden-Breestraat did not check his artistic development. Nor did it keep him from receiving important official commissions. The second *Anatomy Lesson* (figure 20) dates from 1656, and *The Syndics* (page 139) from 1662. In 1661 he was commissioned to execute a large canvas, *The Conspiracy of the Batavians* (page 141). It was rejected and has come down to us only in mutilated form.

It is customary to speak of Rembrandt's work after 1650 as marking a serener period of his art, because he renounced several Baroque compositional devices to which he had resorted immoderately in the 'thirties. But such a view is just as inadequate as that according to which Rembrandt became a master colorist only in his old age. There is only a modicum of truth in each of these views. During the period when his life was tragically overshadowed by external misfortune, Rembrandt remained the same as before, however much his technical means of expression may have changed. In his later works the immanent tension is stronger than before, and the rendering of emotion still more closely interwoven with realistic representation—even though at first glance these works may seem calmer, lighter, clearer than the early ones.

This may be illustrated by *The Anatomy Lesson of Dr. Deyman*, even though only a preliminary sketch of the whole composition and a fragment of the completed work have come down to us (figures 19 and 20). The Governors of the guild of surgeons who surround the demonstrating physician and the corpse are pictured here in a clearer, more severe, classical arrangement; at the same time, the individuals seem to have regained their right to separate characterization. And yet a more powerful effect is attained than in *The Anatomy Lesson* of 1632, by placing the operating anatomist in the center and by rendering the cadaver in a new way. The body, the poor remains of a man used as demonstration for a lesson, is here given in strong foreshortening, on the model of a work by one of Caravaggio's followers, Borgiani, which depicts the lamentation over Christ. Even more incisive, perhaps, is the hideousness of the cadaver with gaping abdomen and opened skull—the physician is exhibiting the pink-colored brain. Through devices of light, shade, and color the demonstrating anatomist to whom the two groups of onlookers at right and left are subordinated has been brought into

17. A RIVER VALLEY WITH RUINS. About 1643–48. Panel, 26 × 33⁷/₈″. *Gemäldegalerie, Cassel*

relief more strikingly, though less shrilly, than in *The Anatomy Lesson of Dr. Tulp*. Moreover, the painting reveals a mastery of technique which far surpasses the artificiality of the earlier composition, and no longer depends on effects of diagonal organization or startling lighting.

All the works of the later years, portraits as well as large historical compositions, show that Rembrandt was not thrown into despair by his misfortunes, but that on the contrary they impelled him to reveal in his work, with understanding and compassion, all that is good and evil in humanity. His paintings are no longer composed as though the beholder were secretly witnessing the action from a hidden corner. Small figures are no longer integrated within great spaces. Everything is now viewed at close quarters, openly and directly—man, his joys, and his sufferings.

During the 'fifties, which were marked by the stress of misfortune and hardship, Rembrandt produced few

landscapes. Instead, we have drawings, and in particular etchings which represent Christ the Comforter in His works and miracles. The great expressive etchings portraying *The Crucifixion* and *The Deposition of Christ* date from 1653 on. Along with these he etched a series illustrating the youth of Christ, for which Titus no doubt served as model.

What strikes us most in these later paintings is the new, impressive color harmonies in his portraits—large, half-length figures placed far to the foreground. In the works of no other artist are the expressive possibilities of color so fully realized. It is enough to mention *The Syndics* (page 139). These unassuming drapers are seated behind a table covered with a red cloth that has yellow threads woven into it. The red of the cloth, in conjunction with the warm brown tones of the background, creates an atmosphere of remarkable grandeur, power, and aloof dignity. The method of individual characterization employed in this painting is related

25

to that used centuries later by Tolstoy and Dostoevsky: the characters are portrayed indirectly, through rendering the details of the environment, which slowly, by a process of accretion, build up a rich and deep life.

18. Drawing for original composition of THE CONSPIRACY OF THE BATAVIANS (see colorplate, page 141). $7^3/_4 \times 7^1/_8''$. *Print Room, Munich*

19. Drawing for THE ANATOMY LESSON OF DR. DEYMAN. 1656. Pen and wash, $4^3/_8 \times 5^1/_4''$. *Rijksmuseum, Amsterdam*

Rembrandt's works oblige us to discard the idea that the color effect of a painting derives only from the application of local color, such as the principal colors of the figures' costumes. These colors, in Rembrandt's works, owe their naturalness mainly to the background painting. Each of these backgrounds is a chaos of colors out of which certain colors emerge and into which others disappear. Rembrandt's contemporaries—Sandrart, for instance—thought that his backgrounds were merely badly painted and much too dark. They did not realize that the inner life of Rembrandt's paintings is largely based on these very backgrounds.

In his early work, the background painting is subdued with many grays (which often appear green where the varnish has turned yellow) and serves as a foil against which the livelier yellows, blues, and reds shine forth. But as Rembrandt's experience of life grew richer, his vision of his environment changed, and the colors changed with it. If there was one thing that he understood better than anyone else, it was how one color may subdue and tame another, or make it break out with explosive force. In many later paintings the background is a warm brown. But we ascribe specific color to one of these backgrounds only by way of abstraction; the actual function of the background is to render the flow of the air as a sort of filler, binding together the multiple tones of color, which only in our memory combine into one color. Rembrandt's backgrounds are generally considered to be brown; but actually his brown is a color that does not merely dim brighter tones, but also makes colors glow again. Rembrandt, the great master of chiaroscuro, who expresses his innermost feelings by means of directed light and shadow, also understood, as hardly anyone else did, the power of colors, and exploited their harmonies and discords. In his old age he applied his colors with far more vigor and emphasis. Those familiar with the art of his period are amazed at the way colors then fashionable in women's dress—deep red and salmon pink, for example—suddenly acquire full emotional significance in Rembrandt.

It was in his old age that Rembrandt produced the works that are so notable for the shattering vehemence of their colors. However great the disposition to calm and harmony that these pictures reveal (by the use of complementary reds and greens, for instance), they are animated by the greatest tension. For Rembrandt has put a certain distance between his reds and greens, and wherever he has used them as vehicles of a particular meaning, he has interposed yellows and blues. No one has equaled Rembrandt in the ability to make a yellow glow brilliantly through the slightest nuance, or at other moments to transform it into a poor muddy

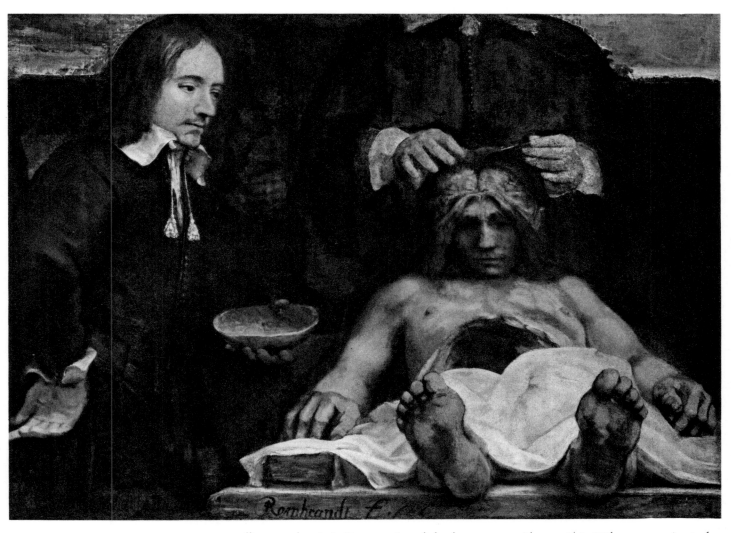

20. THE ANATOMY LESSON OF DR. DEYMAN (fragment). 1656. Canvas; size of the fragment, 39³/₈ × 52³/₄″. *Rijksmuseum, Amsterdam*

color. There is a great wealth of expressive possibilities in his blues, which range from a light blue to a blue that has almost the glow of an emerald green. We are referring primarily to the historical paintings of the late period, with their large-sized figures, but the same observations apply also to the portraits where the range of colors seems more limited. In these later portraits, however, the various elements of character, dramatic situation, and human vision are much more closely interrelated than in his earlier works. Each of them transcends its time and circumstances. These late works, and most particularly the two group portraits (pages 147 and 149) which date probably from the last years of Rembrandt's life, are a riot of color such as nature exhibits only in her autumnal ripeness: the contrasting hues of sunny days in late fall. In *The Prodigal Son* (page 149), for example, the colors with their overtones of suffering and compassion attract and are bound up in one another. Through such coloristic devices, Rembrandt suggests serene acceptance, reconciliation with life.

That such a work should have been painted at the close of Rembrandt's life is surely symbolic. Death had taken a heavy toll around him in the last decades, and it would not be surprising if it had broken his power to record the sufferings of man with such warmth, and his faith that despite everything life is a worthwhile experience. In the last year of his life, in 1669, Rembrandt stands essentially alone as the painter whose subject has always been humanity, even when he paints his own features, those of a simple man. His last self-portrait (page 151) is deeply moving in its subdued colorfulness. He records himself and the world with the whole *furioso* of his color, his light, and his line. The solitary artist, who all his life wanted only to do full justice to man with all man's sufferings and errors, accepts these with serenity, humanity, and courage.

It is clear that an art of this kind must necessarily know periods of appreciation and periods of condemnation, according to man's ability to feel human and free as a member of the family of mankind.

ETCHINGS

The catalogue numbers of Rembrandt's etchings in this section are preceded by the letters Mz. and refer to the numbers given in
Rembrandt's Etchings: Reproductions of the Whole Original Etched Work,
edited by Ludwig Münz. London, Phaidon Press, 1952. 2 vols.

REMBRANDT'S etchings were intended, if you will, to have a wide distribution amongst the general public; and in this they differ from his drawings, which constitute the most delicate, the most irreplaceable side of his art.

In contrast to the line engraver, who must slowly incise or dig out each line, the etcher can work fast. With his etching needle he can draw his design into the protective wax coating on his copper plate as easily as he draws with a pencil on paper. The stroke of the needle scratches off part of the protective coat, exposing the metal; and the lines thus produced are bitten—or etched—into the plate by acid. When the etching is completed, the protective layer of wax is removed, the plate is inked, and prints are then pulled. The effect of the etched line is quite different from that of the engraved line whose width varies according to the strength with which the burin is applied to the copper. For this reason, each individual line in an etching is perhaps less expressive; but the technique of multiple layers and deep acid treatments of entire complexes of strokes affords nuances of dark—and

hence of light—that could not be achieved by any other previously known procedure.

This is not the place for a detailed discussion of how Rembrandt learned etching technique and made the etching needle an obedient instrument for his artistic purposes. We shall merely observe that it was only after several years of experimentation—his earliest undated prints were produced about 1626, and the earliest dated prints in 1628—that he discovered the expressive potentialities and technique of etching suitable to his genius. This was around 1630. From then on he produced an uninterrupted series of studies and portraits, and above all, Biblical compositions, in which he recorded reality in his own unique manner, as though accidentally surprising it, and yet making us experience the great emotional force of his interpretations of the Bible.

His etchings, like his drawings, reveal a gradual development. As we have indicated in our introduction, before Rembrandt achieved chiaroscuro effects in his paintings he often obtained them in his etchings by means of broad, loosely placed strokes which pro-

21. THE WOMAN WITH THE ARROW.
Signed and dated: Rembrandt f. 1661.
8 × 4⁷/₈″. Mz. 144. State II.
The Pierpont Morgan Library, New York

dom in this medium in the portrait studies of the 'thirties, whereas in his Biblical compositions he adhered to the exaggerated Baroque pattern until about 1639. *The Death of the Virgin* of 1639 is a subject in which he freely used the dry point technique—that is, he used his needle to gouge the lines directly into the plate instead of etching them with acid. This print marks the approximate date when etching became for Rembrandt a means for expressing things that could not have been expressed in any other medium. To be sure, etching had been practiced as a distinct art in Italy before him, but it was only with Rembrandt and through him that it developed into a genuine artistic medium. From Rembrandt's etchings dated after 1640 a straight line leads through Goya to that period of etching whose most typical representative was Whistler.

Whereas many etched scenes from the Old and the New Testaments, dating from the 'thirties, such as the large *Raising of Lazarus* and almost all the compositions of this type up to the *Death of the Virgin* are, so to speak, black-and-white reproductions of paintings, the etchings Rembrandt produced after 1640 are the purest examples of this unique art, owing their vitality exclusively to the colorful force and richness of their embossed dark lines.

From the 'forties date a series of Rembrandt's most famous etchings, including *The Three Trees* (figure 31) and *Christ Healing the Sick* (figure 32, called "The Hundred Guilder Print," because even in Rembrandt's lifetime copies of it sold for the high price of one

duce an illusion of reality permeated with light and shadows. It must be noted, however, that he at first achieved mastery of etching technique by working with small-sized prints. For large prints he resorted to collaborators as late as the second half of the 'thirties. *The Raising of Lazarus* (figure 28), *The Good Samaritan*, *The Descent from the Cross*, and *Ecce Homo* are the best-known examples of such collaboration. Rembrandt used etchers for these works for the same reason that Rubens used his line engravers: he regarded his etchings as a mere means for reproducing pictorial compositions in black and white. But Rembrandt's ability to render the richness of light effects and to create spatial depth by means of lights and darks radically distinguishes his etchings from the works of the Rubens engravers. He first achieved complete free-

22. REMBRANDT'S MOTHER.
Signed and dated (in State II): RHL 1628.
2⁵/₈ × 2¹/₂″. Mz. 82. State II.
The Pierpont Morgan Library, New York

29

hundred guilder). His etching style, just as his painting style changed, became more grandiose, more monumental after 1650. During the 'fifties he etched a series of scenes illustrating the story of Christ. In this decade, in addition to the etching needle, the dry point needle played an increasingly crucial part, allowing him to cut broad lines in the plate, to work faster and more directly. These compositions mark the classical apotheosis of Rembrandt's etching art. The most beautiful etched landscapes date from the early 'fifties. Then, in 1653, a new change occurs, related to Rembrandt's unhappy personal experiences: from that moment on, human suffering once again becomes almost exclusively his subject matter. This period opens with the magnificent dry point, *The Three Crosses*. What a change from the intimate style of the *St. Jerome* or the *Faust* (figure 34) that he had created shortly before! Finally, 1654 brings us the deeply moving cycle depicting the youth of Christ, and 1655, *Christ Presented to the People* with its many states. These successive states are not—as they often were with earlier artists—a mere matter of removing certain lines or adding others for the sake of improving the original composition; instead, they became entirely new in their artistic effect.

But with the introduction of the mixed technique, plates became less durable; their full beauty could be reproduced only in the best prints—prints for which Rembrandt used silky China paper when he found it appropriate. The dry point wears off at a faster rate than the etching, and the artistic value decreases when the lines made with the dry point needle become too thin, and instead of the deep, wide, and irregular dark burr of the strokes, we have an effect of brightness without character.

Rembrandt's last etchings, such as *The Three Crosses* in the fourth state, which move us so deeply, are thus again works of art as unique as his drawings or paintings, and actually are not suited for reproduction. After 1660 Rembrandt was no longer interested in appealing to a larger public by means of etchings, and he produced only isolated prints. His portrait of Van Linden, professor of botany, dating from 1665, is his latest extant etching. In the final decade of his life, Rembrandt, to a far greater extent than ever before, was essentially a painter, as may be seen in the thickly inked effects of these etchings when they are viewed in the proper light. Good proofs of these works, not altered by false restoration, are surely among his most significant and most human creations.

23. BEGGAR WITH A CRIPPLED HAND.
About 1628–29.
$3^7/_8 \times 1^5/_8''$. Mz. 106. State I.
The Pierpont Morgan Library, New York

24. OLD BEGGAR WOMAN WITH
A GOURD. About 1628–29.
$4^1/_8 \times 1^3/_4''$. Mz. 107. State II.
The Pierpont Morgan Library, New York

30

25. REMBRANDT BAREHEADED.
Signed: RHL 1629 (in reverse). 7 × 6¹/₁₆″. Mz. 3. *Print Room, Amsterdam*

26. SHEET OF STUDIES: HEAD OF REMBRANDT,
BEGGAR COUPLE, HEAD OF OLD MAN AND OLD WOMAN.
About 1630. $3^7/_8 \times 4''$. Mz. 13. State II.
The Pierpont Morgan Library, New York

27. CHRIST DISPUTING WITH THE DOCTORS.
1630.
$3^1/_2 \times 2^5/_8''$. Mz. 190. State III.
The Pierpont Morgan Library, New York

32

28. THE RAISING OF LAZARUS. About 1630–31. 14$^{1}/_{2}$ × 10$^{1}/_{8}$″. Mz. 192. State V. *British Museum, London*

29. REMBRANDT AND HIS WIFE SASKIA.
Signed and dated: Rembrandt f. 1636.
$4\,^1/_8 \times 3\,^3/_4''$. Mz. 21. State I.
The Pierpont Morgan Library, New York

30. THE RETURN OF THE
PRODIGAL SON.
Signed and dated:
Rembrandt f. 1636.
$6\,^1/_8 \times 5\,^3/_8''$. Mz. 207.
The Pierpont Morgan Library,
New York

31. THE THREE TREES. Signed and dated: Rembrandt f. 1643. 8¹/₄ × 11″. Mz. 152. *The Pierpont Morgan Library, New York*

32. CHRIST HEALING THE SICK (THE HUNDRED GUILDER PRINT). About 1642–45. 11 × 15⁵/₈″. Mz. 217. State II.
The Pierpont Morgan Library, New York

33. EPHRAIM BONUS, JEWISH PHYSICIAN.
Signed and dated, below, right (hardly visible): Rembrandt f. 1647. 9³/₈ × 7″. Mz. 69. State II.
The Pierpont Morgan Library, New York

34. FAUST IN HIS STUDY, WATCHING A MAGIC DISK.
About 1652–53. $8\,^1/_4 \times 6\,^3/_8''$. Mz. 275. State II. *The Pierpont Morgan Library, New York*

35. THE FLIGHT INTO EGYPT.
Signed and dated: Rembrandt f. 1654. $3^3/_4 \times 5^5/_8''$. Mz. 228.
The Pierpont Morgan Library, New York

36. THE VIRGIN AND CHILD WITH THE CAT, AND JOSEPH AT THE WINDOW.
Signed and dated: Rembrandt f. 1654. $3^3/_4 \times 5^5/_8''$. Mz. 229. State II.
The Pierpont Morgan Library, New York

37. CHRIST SEATED DISPUTING WITH THE DOCTORS.
Signed and dated: Rembrandt f. 1654. 3 ³/₄ × 5 ⁵/₈″. Mz. 230. State II.
The Pierpont Morgan Library, New York

38. CHRIST BETWEEN HIS PARENTS, RETURNING FROM THE TEMPLE.
Signed and dated: Rembrandt f. 1654. 3 ³/₄ × 5 ⁵/₈″. Mz. 231.
The Pierpont Morgan Library, New York

39. ABRAHAM'S SACRIFICE.
Signed and dated: Rembrandt f. 1655.
$6^1/_8 \times 5^1/_8$". Mz. 184.
The Pierpont Morgan Library, New York

40. ABRAHAM ENTERTAINING THE ANGELS.
Signed and dated: Rembrandt f. 1656.
$6^3/_8 \times 5^1/_8$". Mz. 185.
The Pierpont Morgan Library, New York

41. THE PHOENIX, OR THE STATUE OVERTHROWN.
Signed and dated, right, below: Rembrandt f. 1658. $7^1/_8 \times 7^3/_{16}''$. Mz. 279. *The Pierpont Morgan Library, New York*

REMBRANDT'S
DRAWINGS

42. PILATE WASHING HIS HANDS.
Pen and wash heightened with white.
About 1665. 5⁷/₈ × 7¹/₄″.
British Museum, London

43. FARM BUILDINGS.
Pen and wash.
About 1650. 4¹/₈ × 6¹/₂″.
Akademische Gemäldegalerie, Vienna

REMBRANDT'S drawings and etchings met with general recognition even in his lifetime—indeed, somewhat earlier than his paintings; and they upheld his reputation as a brilliant portrayer of Biblical subjects in his later period when his paintings were rejected by classicists because of his thickly encrusted pigment. It is above all thanks to his drawings and etchings that Rembrandt the painter was rediscovered as early as the end of the seventeenth century, with the writings of the French amateur, Roger de Piles. From then on, except for a few short intervals, his fame has steadily grown.

Rembrandt's drawings are perhaps the most authentic documents of his art. Although they were often quickly penned on small sheets of paper that he happened to have at hand, they are works of art in the full sense of the word. To an even greater extent than in the case of his paintings, the charm and full significance of his drawings can be grasped only by a thorough study of the originals; even the best reproductions cannot serve as substitutes. What we see in the reproductions gives us only a rough idea of the human message conveyed by the originals, and of the amazing effects of his chiaroscuro saturated with the fullness of life. Incidentally, the etchings too show only in the best prints what Rembrandt actually wanted to express in them; their artistic value decreases as the plates wear out, and contrasts become dulled. Much the same may be said of Rembrandt's drawings, those subtlest products of his art, whose charm can no longer be sensed when the paper yellows with the passage of time, or when they are blemished by stains.

Rembrandt drew throughout his life. His work—both paintings and etchings—actually arose out of countless rapidly sketched drawings in which he observed his surroundings. The young Rembrandt's first drawings are marked by adherence to the prevalent tradition: he was strongly influenced in the manner of making his strokes by everything he learned from artists as different as Lastman, Callot, and Blomaert. Even in these earliest drawings the stroke is vigorous, and the accents are placed by means of wash; but although they display brilliant directness and unsparing observation, to the layman they may suggest a primitive groping. It took time before Rembrandt found himself, before he became the great draftsman we admire today. From the very outset we have this impulsive manner of sketching with only a few strokes, which at the same time produce for us—and therein largely lies his significance as a draftsman—the impression of the quickly seen, of the typical moment grasped and forever fixed on paper in its unexpected truth. In addition to the studies of figures in chalk and red chalk, we must above all mention here the pen drawings with their uncannily deft washes: a crucial example of this manner is the magnificent and yet so unemotionally conceived sketch of *Christ Carrying the Cross* (figure 48) dating from the early 'thirties. But however effective these drawings may be, Rembrandt himself regarded most of them as preliminary sketches, something that he recorded with the intention of using it later for his paintings or etchings. We know from the auction

inventory of 1656 that, like every other painter of that time, he kept his sketches classified in groups—figures, landscapes, architecture, studies after ancient models, et cetera.

Those cycles of drawings which were particularly appreciated in the eighteenth century for their inventiveness, whether they represent landscapes or Biblical scenes, date chiefly from a later period, after 1640. Rembrandt's style of drawing slowly and steadily acquired greatness, while preserving realism no matter how small the sheet of paper. The main group of the drawings representing Christ, His miracles and His passion, dates from the 'fifties. It was then that he actually produced his most stirring drawings in the broad style of his late period, related to the style of his paintings. At that time he also began to use a new instrument for drawing, which helped him to obtain entirely new effects, unique in their spontaneity: this is the reed pen, with its broad variable stroke, which he preferred to the quill pen with its more delicate and more uniform strokes; similarly, the 'fifties are marked by his increasing use of the dry point needle in his etchings. Moreover, after 1650 his choice of paper is masterly. On the basic tone of the paper (in the landscapes too the paper is often tinted) the misty, delicate washes have a coloristic force equal to that of his late paintings. From the 'sixties, the last decade of his life, there have been preserved only a very few drawings, broadly executed with the reed pen, and marked by a power which is truly extraordinary.

44. SELF-PORTRAIT. Pen and wash.
About 1628–29. 5 × 3 ³/₄″.
British Museum, London

45. SELF-PORTRAIT. Pen and ink wash.
Signed and dated: RHL 1630. 3 ¹/₈ × 3 ³/₄″.
The Louvre, Paris

46. ST. PETER STANDING. Black chalk. About 1630. 10 × 7 1/2″. *Print Room, Dresden*

47. A MAN IN A HIGH CAP, WITH FOLDED HANDS.
Pen and bistre with slight washes of white. About 1632–33. 6⅝ × 5⅛″.
British Museum, London

48. CHRIST CARRYING THE CROSS. Pen and wash. About 1635–36. $5^5/_8 \times 10^1/_8$". *Print Room, Berlin*

49. CHRIST WITH MARY AND MARTHA. Pen and wash. About 1643. $6^5/_8 \times 9^1/_4''$. *British Museum, London*

50. A HOUSE AMID TREES ON THE BANK OF A RIVER. Pen and wash. About 1646. $6^{1}/_{4} \times 9^{1}/_{8}$″. *British Museum, London*

51. CANAL AND TOWPATH. Brush and sepia. About 1654–55. 4 $^1/_8$ × 7 $^3/_8$″. *Ashmolean Museum, Oxford*

52. SELF-PORTRAIT, FULL LENGTH.
Pen and wash. About 1652–53. 8 × 5 1/4″. *Rembrandt House, Amsterdam*

53. FOUR ORIENTALS SEATED BENEATH A TREE.
Pen and wash on Japanese paper. About 1655–56. 7⁵/₈ × 5″. *British Museum, London*

54. HAGAR AND ISHMAEL IN THE DESERT. Pen and wash. About 1654–55. 7¹/₈ × 9⁵/₈". *Kunsthalle, Hamburg*

55. CHRIST BAPTIZED IN THE JORDAN. Pen, slightly washed. About 1656–60. $6\frac{1}{2} \times 9\frac{7}{8}''$. *Print Room, Dresden*

56. CHRIST AND THE WOMAN TAKEN IN ADULTERY. Pen, partly washed with red and gray. About 1659. $6^3/_4 \times 8''$.
Print Room, Munich

57. THE LAMENTATION OVER CHRIST. Pen and wash. About 1655–57. 5⁷/₈ × 7⁵/₈″. *Print Room, Berlin*

58. HOMER DICTATING HIS VERSES.
Pen and wash. About 1663. $5^3/_4 \times 6^1/_2''$. *Nationalmuseum, Stockholm*

COLORPLATES

Painted 1626

THE ANGEL AND THE PROPHET BALAAM

Oil on wood, 25¹/₄ × 18¹/₂″

Musée Cognacq-Jay, Paris

This is one of Rembrandt's earliest historical paintings. As is the case with all of his Biblical compositions, one must consult the text on which it is based in order fully to understand what he created by means of line and color. In Numbers XXII we find the story of how Balak, king of the Moabites, asked the prophet Balaam to curse the people of Israel, and how God transformed this curse into a blessing. Rembrandt shows us the crucial scene: Balaam, who does not perceive that an angel of the Lord stands in his way, smites his ass. The beast in its predicament begins to speak, and at this moment Balaam realizes that he must heed the voice of God and of His messenger.

The composition, though recalling Caravaggio, may still be regarded as unmistakably academic: the prophet, painted in motley luminous colors, is placed in the center. But even in this youthful work, Rembrandt introduces a second focus of interest, which perhaps strikes us still more forcefully: the tormented beast which knows the way better than its rider. The gray head of the speaking ass stands out in strong contrast against the angel's white garment. It is also interesting to note in this early work that Rembrandt, who so often tries to present the Biblical text in realistic terms, has placed the angel with his sword where Balaam actually cannot see him. Finally, one may add that it is in keeping with Rembrandt's realism and his characteristic use of light and dark to show the secondary figures, such as the servants or the rich Moabite princes accompanying Balaam, either at some distance or entirely in the shadow.

Painted about 1628–29

SIMEON IN THE TEMPLE

Oil on wood, 22 × 17″

Kunsthalle, Hamburg

This painting, with its large, strongly lighted figures, quite properly belongs to the end of Rembrandt's Caravaggiesque period. From it we may have a real insight into his painting and thinking, and into his growing power of expression through color, light and dark.

Here, too, it is important to recall the subject matter. The aged Simeon has come to the temple wishing, before his death, to see the future Redeemer. The scene represents the moment when Simeon, full of gratitude, holds the child Jesus in his arms and kneels as he announces his message to Mary. Deeply moved, she also is kneeling, her hands clasped. Her face expresses astonishment as well as knowledge of what will come to pass. Quite in the foreground, where the colors are most earthy, Joseph is seen on his knees praying. Above them, with a powerful gesture, stands Anna, the aged widow who, like Simeon, served faithfully and was given the privilege of seeing the Redeemer. She is shown raising her arms in thanks to the Lord.

This painting reveals progress in Rembrandt's ability to create a striking effect of real life by means of contrasts between linear structure and color: Anna, who bears the features of Rembrandt's mother, is the apex of the triangular composition of the group; but at the same time our eyes are directed—through the color scheme—to the little Child surrounded by the luminous aura, the future Redeemer.

Painted about 1629

SELF-PORTRAIT

Oil on wood, 14³/₄ × 11³/₈″

Mauritshuis, The Hague

Few painters have made so many self-portraits as Rembrandt. The first one dates from about 1626, when he was twenty years old, the last (page 151) from shortly before his death, when he was sixty-two or sixty-three. It is a unique experience to be able in this way to follow the physical appearance of a painter almost from year to year. But the changes in his features are not of greatest interest to us; more important is the way in which he portrayed himself, making it possible for us to fathom something of his essential being. An artist does not receive commissions for self-portraits. They are paintings in which he is entirely free and alone with himself, in the full sense of the phrase.

The self-portrait here reproduced is the first that is truly a portrait. Those that preceded it were merely studies of light and dark, or of certain facial expressions. Here we see Rembrandt for the first time looking at the world with some self-confidence. The portrait must have been painted about 1629, after several years of intense self-training in Leyden, where he worked with his friend Jan Lievens. The words which the erudite and art-minded Constantijn Huygens wrote in his autobiography (in Latin) about the two young painters seem directly applicable to this portrait: "The son of the embroiderer is named Jan Lievens; the son of the miller, Rembrandt. Both are still beardless and, in face and figure, more children than young men." In view of this comment, Huygens' great admiration for their work is to be applauded.

Rembrandt's paintings from his Leyden period are usually small and are painted with great care and precision, but in all of them the play of light and dark that so strongly engrossed him throughout his life is abundantly evident. [B.H.]

Painted about 1630

THE RAISING OF LAZARUS

Oil on wood, 37¹/₂ × 32¹/₂"

Collection Howard F. Ahmanson, Los Angeles

Throughout his life, Rembrandt returned to the subject of the raising of Lazarus, because it gave him the opportunity for the pictorial expression of two ideas. On the one hand, the theme is the divine power to resurrect and redeem. Contrasted with this is the second theme—the behavior of a human being when consciousness returns to him. In devotional pictures of this subject, Lazarus, resurrected by faith after being entombed for three days, turns gratefully to Christ. But Rembrandt represents him as a man who, though he has just awakened from death, acts only as though he has been awakened from a deep slumber, and cannot understand what is happening around him.

The painting preceded the etching (see figure 28) in which Christ's appearance is even more powerful: he is seen with his back half-turned in such a way that the beholder is, so to speak, made a part of the picture. In the painting the beholder is imaginatively placed near one of Lazarus' sisters in the corner, facing Christ. Like all of Rembrandt's works after 1629, this painting discloses something new: it is space with its darkness which primarily conveys the emotion of the picture. The human figures are subordinated. Here Christ is standing near the tomb; the brightest light falls from one side on the spectators and then on Lazarus, and from the darkness there rises Christ's arm with its gesture of divine power.

Painted 1631

SIMEON IN THE TEMPLE

Oil on wood, 24 × 18⁷/₈″

Mauritshuis, The Hague

This *Simeon in the Temple* reveals, to a far greater extent than the *Lazarus*, Rembrandt's mastery of the potentialities of chiaroscuro. Here, the whole scene is subordinated to space, yet the emotional impact of this painting equals or even surpasses that of the *Lazarus*. The subject of this painting is the same as that of the painting dating from 1628–29 (page 61); yet how much more quietly everything is rendered here! No trace is left of Baroque pathos—that is to say, the flamboyant show of emotion. Rembrandt's ability to transform the accidental, passing moment into a memorable, experienced truth has in the meantime greatly increased.

The painting shows a high room in the temple; a beam of light hits the group of Simeon with the Child, which the prophetess approaches with her hand lifted in blessing. The brightest light in the dark space of this large synagogue falls on Simeon holding the Redeemer in his arms, and on Mary in light blue, who kneels beside him. Even to a greater extent than before color has acquired the power to render the forms naturalistically and to keep them knit firmly together. Here Rembrandt obtains such an effect of naturalness through the way in which the yellowish glints of light on the pillar just behind Simeon are scratched out from the darker parts; as a result the pillar helps to emphasize the central group.

The whole curiosity of the youthful Rembrandt bent on grasping life is expressed here. He shows us an extraordinary event taking place amidst the normal bustle of existence, between figures who walk about in the temple and disappear in the darkness, and other figures who reverently climb the steps leading to the high priest dimly seen under the canopy.

66

Painted 1632

THE ANATOMY LESSON OF DR. TULP

Oil on canvas, 65 × 86¹/₂"

Mauritshuis, The Hague

This painting was Rembrandt's first important commission for a group portrait, and it may have been one of the reasons for his moving to Amsterdam. It shows Dr. Tulp demonstrating the muscles of the forearm with the help of the famous textbook by Vesalius which stands at the feet of the corpse. Since the restoration of the painting we may now see more distinctly a drawing of this forearm on the sheet of paper inscribed also with the names of the surgeons.

Only now, through this latest restoration, has the coherent arrangement of the figures in depth been revealed. Dr. Tulp and his listeners, all of them portrayed at close range, now exist in a convincing atmospheric space which Rembrandt accomplishes through chiaroscuro; and we perceive fully the contrast between the tones of the corpse and the vivid colors of the physicians who follow the lecturer's demonstration with various degrees of attentiveness. The whole scene is intense and dramatic, and the action of lecturing is represented so strikingly that mere portraiture recedes in importance. Dr. Tulp's hands are in the brightest light: one lifts a strand of muscles with a scalpel, while the other performs an explanatory gesture. This results in a new focus of interest, since the dark red muscles stand out against the colors of the corpse.

It is amazing how Rembrandt subordinates everything to his main theme. We are drawn into the circle of those present, we are very close, just in front of the physicians in the foreground. Since the restoration, the structure of the group seems less dense. Instead of the over-all dark mass, the physicians' clothes are now varied but still subdued in color. As a result, the linear pattern of this group, the classical triangular composition, loses much of its insistence, so that it impresses us only as a living contrast to the strongest colors—the red of the muscles— in the central area. Such over-refined, almost manneristic playing with linear composition actually contributes to the realism of the scene: the figures, with Dr. Tulp in the center, represented as helper and teacher, are linked together in the liveliest way by the chiaroscuro and the colors.

Painted about 1632–33

THE RAISING OF THE CROSS

Oil on canvas, 37³/₄ × 28³/₈″

Pinakothek, Munich

A Passion series for Stadholder Frederick Henry, Prince of Orange, was Rembrandt's second important commission (the first was *The Anatomy Lesson of Dr. Tulp*, 1632; page 69). There is no doubt that Constantijn Huygens, secretary to the prince and a great admirer of the young Rembrandt's work, was the prime mover behind this order. Rembrandt at once got busy, and within a short time had painted and delivered *The Raising of the Cross* and *The Descent from the Cross* (page 73). Then he slowed down and could not seem to finish the three other pieces—*The Entombment*, *The Resurrection*, and *The Ascension*. Not until 1639 was the series completed. In 1646 he added an *Adoration of the Shepherds* and a *Circumcision* to the five Passion scenes. The last-named has disappeared; the other six paintings are now in Munich.

Rembrandt's long dilly dallying was fortunate for posterity: it occasioned a correspondence between him and Huygens that has been preserved and forms one of the rare original sources on this elusive human being who painted but did not write. Most important, the letters contain some of Rembrandt's few comments on his own work. Upon delivering *The Entombment* and *The Resurrection* in 1639, he wrote: " . . . for these show the greatest and most natural movement, and that is also the main reason they took me so long to finish."

It is remarkable, and perhaps also typical of the painter, that he portrayed himself in both *The Raising of the Cross* and *The Descent from the Cross*. In the former, he is the soldier in blue, with a beret on his head, who is helping to set up the cross. In the latter, he is the figure, again in blue, standing on the ladder and helping to hold the body of Christ. [B.H.]

70

Painted about 1633–34

THE DESCENT FROM THE CROSS

Oil on wood, 35¹/₂ × 22″

Pinakothek, Munich

The scene takes place under a dark nocturnal sky; but a ray of light has pierced it, vividly focused on the diagonally placed cross in the center. The blood glows red on the brown wood. The rest of the scene is enveloped in such darkness that we become aware only slowly of the presence of the other figures, whose positions, in a manner characteristic of Rembrandt, express the most varied feelings. At the right a figure in deep brown-red somberly witnesses the scene; this probably represents Nicodemus who received permission to bury the Savior. At the left in the foreground is Mary, whose colors are hardly visible in the deep shadows. She is shown fainting and supported by the women. In the background we can see the apostles standing in the shadow. The livid color of Christ's body, set off against the white linen, produces a unique, unforgettable effect, which is further enhanced by the vigorous tones of the surrounding figures—the red and yellow of the apostle below who receives the corpse, and the strong blue of the stooping man on the ladder who bears Rembrandt's features. The man at the top holds the winding sheet and grips the cross, emphasizing the action of lowering the body.

Two emotions expressed in Rembrandt's etching of the same scene are conveyed in this painting just as strikingly by means of effects of light. The strongly realistic livid tones of the corpse and Christ's face distorted by agony arouse our compassion, while the bright colors of the apostles who receive Christ's body and the sharply tapering triangle of the winding sheet produce a light, which in conjunction with the glowing cross, arouses an emotion that is almost the opposite of compassion—a feeling of authentic deliverance.

Painted in 1633

THE STORM ON THE SEA OF GALILEE

Oil on canvas, 63 × 50"

Isabella Stewart Gardner Museum, Boston

Portraits and Biblical themes were by far Rembrandt's favorite subjects for his paintings. He seldom painted landscapes, and in contrast to the views of the polders around Amsterdam so often appearing in his etchings and drawings, the landscapes in his paintings are usually fanciful and dramatic. Nor does he seem to have shared other Dutch artists' love of seascapes. Therefore this depiction of the Bible story in which Christ and his disciples are overtaken by a storm while crossing the Sea of Galilee is of unusual interest, for it is Rembrandt's only sea painting, although the sea is of course not the major subject. That, to Rembrandt, was clearly the representation of human emotions in the face of nature's violence.

When he painted this canvas, in 1633, he spectacularly achieved the effect he was after. The wildness of the storm thrilled him and gave him full opportunity to transform the desperate struggles of the disciples into one powerful surge of movement, with the calm figure of Christ forming a strong contrast to, and the only resting point in, the turbulence. For a realistic detail, he introduced a seasick disciple.

It is possible that Rembrandt followed a composition by Marten de Vos as model for this painting. [B.H.]

74

Painted in 1635

SAMSON THREATENING HIS FATHER-IN-LAW

Oil on canvas, 61³/₈ × 50³/₄"

State Museums, Berlin-Dahlem

Between 1635 and 1641 Rembrandt painted four large canvases with subjects from the Bible story of Samson in the Book of Judges. These were: *Samson Threatening His Father-in-Law* (1635), *The Blinding of Samson* (1636, page 79), *Samson's Wedding Feast* (1638), and *The Sacrifice of Manoah* (1641). It is characteristic of Rembrandt's development that he first painted the more flamboyant themes and ended with the most intimate: the angel's announcement of Samson's birth to Manoah and his wife.

In this canvas, the earliest of the series, Samson is clad in a rich damask coat and wears a short ornamented sword at his waist; he clenches his fist in powerless fury at his red-capped father-in-law, who looks dazedly down from the window. That this painting was originally larger is known from an old copy showing, at the left, two young Negro slaves (only one of whom is now visible) holding a kid. The full version therefore provided positive identification of the subject, for Judges 15 : 1 says: "But it came to pass within a while after, in the time of the wheat harvest, that Samson visited his wife with a kid; and he said, I will go in to my wife into the chamber. But her father would not suffer him to go in," having given his daughter to another man. Samson's anger had every justification. Why Rembrandt gave Samson his own facial features is not clear. By 1635 his own father-in-law had been dead for several years, so that fortunately we need not seek a parallel with his own life.

Although some parts of this canvas are beautifully painted, and the light effects are impressive—the shadow of the fist on the wall seems a predecessor of the shadow of Captain Banning Cocq's hand on his lieutenant's tunic in *The Night Watch* (page 93)—this work nevertheless betrays a certain awkwardness, an incomplete control of the large surface, so that Samson's anger is less cosmic than comic. [B.H.]

76

Painted 1636

THE BLINDING OF SAMSON

Oil on canvas, 95 × 114¹/₂″

Städelsches Kunstinstitut, Frankfurt

One of the most magnificent of Rembrandt's large Baroque compositions, this painting dates from the period of his greatest prosperity and worldly success. It shows Delilah escaping with the shorn locks of the hero whose strength she has betrayed, while he is blinded by the Philistines. Saskia, Rembrandt's young wife, served as the model for Delilah—a fact that has often been noted.

The act of betrayal, and the brutal mutilation of a hero, are strikingly expressed in this painting by the sheer impact of colors. Instead of merely recording a fragment of reality, color here serves unexpectedly as the major vehicle of dramatic action. At first it might seem that the artist was bent only on recording the reality of the scene and the light that comes in through the opening in the dark, rich drapery of the luxurious room. In the half-light, the Philistines, summoned by the treacherous woman, fetter and blind Samson. The opening through which Delilah escapes is dramatically lighted, and the full brilliance of the light falls on her hands, the one with the locks and the other with the scissors. The light blue, lemon yellow, and grayish tones attract the beholder's attention. But this brightness serves also to emphasize Samson's foot and leg which no longer can strike with force at his betrayer. The over-bright colors of Samson's garment, the dull grays, and the blandness of the yellow form a haunting contrast to the powerful red of the warrior at the left.

Here Rembrandt has once again exploited the counterpoint of linear and color composition, to stress the vividness of the whole. Triumphant Delilah forms the apex of the triangular composition, with the blinded hero as its base, but the latter has become a second—but actual—center of the painting, by means of the colors that hold us spellbound. This savagely intense painting with its horror-inspiring realism and its use of color is one of Rembrandt's most demonic, most gripping works.

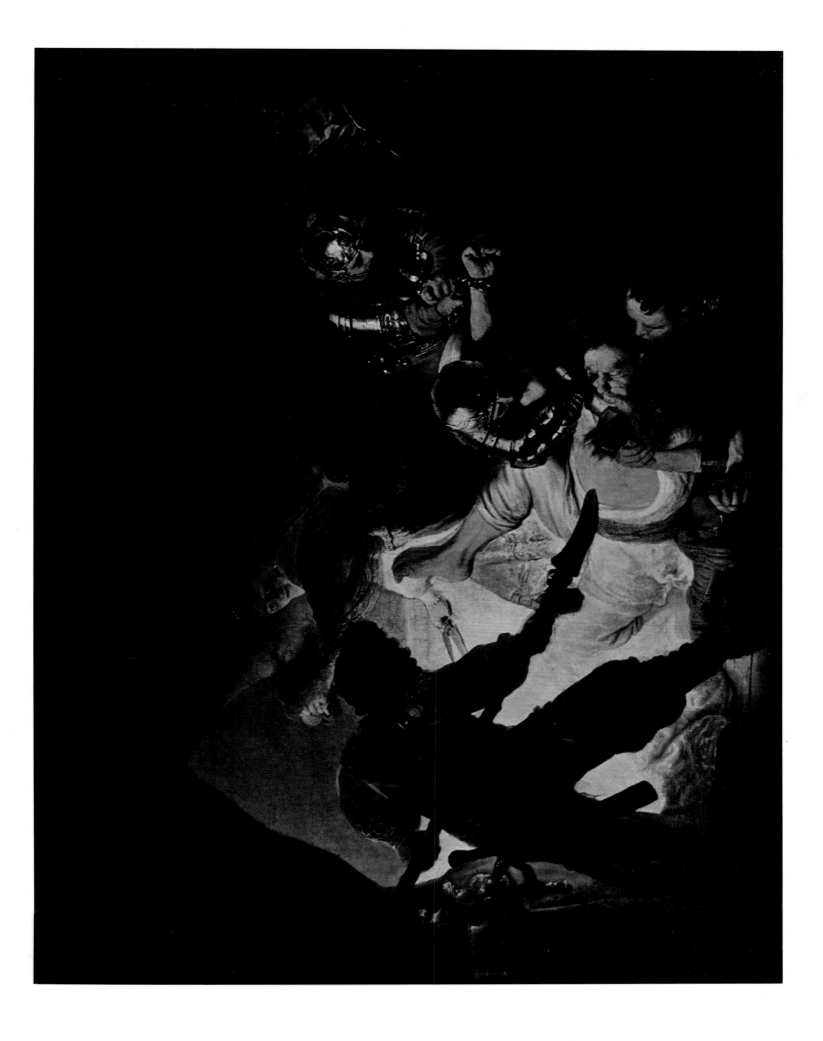

Painted in 1636

DANAË

Oil on canvas, 72⁷/₈ × 79³/₄″
The Hermitage, Leningrad

The *Danaë* in the Hermitage at Leningrad is unquestionably one of Rembrandt's greatest creations. The viewer is overwhelmed by the magnificent painting style and by the intimate beauty of a nude woman ready to receive her lover.

The canvas has been called variously "Rachel Awaiting Jacob," "Venus Awaiting Mars," "Hagar Awaiting Abraham," "Leah Awaiting Jacob"—a matter of preferential identification that leaves the basic subject intact. Yet it can be assumed that Rembrandt here intended to portray Danaë, daughter of Acrisius, King of Argos, who was put into strict and virginal confinement by her father because the oracle had told him he would die at the hand of his grandson. Undeterred by man-made barriers, Zeus visits Danaë in the form of a shower of gold, and she bears their son, Perseus.

Most artists painting the Danaë theme lavished attention on the shower of gold, making their pictures easy to identify. Rembrandt, however, omits it, merely suggesting the arrival of Zeus by the light at the left and by the old servant holding open the draperies. Floating above Danaë, and symbolizing her enforced isolation, is a weeping cupid with bound hands.

Recent research has revealed that, years after finishing the painting in 1636, Rembrandt touched it up at various points. This casts new light on an earlier surmise that the canvas in the Hermitage is the same as that listed in the 1656 inventory of Rembrandt's possessions as "A large work, called Danaë." If this is indeed so, it probably means that Rembrandt had kept the painting for himself, that it was one of his own favorites, and that he lost it at the sale of his property following his bankruptcy. [B.H.]

80

Painted 1637

THE ANGEL DEPARTING FROM THE FAMILY OF TOBIAS

Oil on wood, $26^3/_4 \times 20^1/_2''$

The Louvre, Paris

Recently restored, this painting once again glows in Rembrandt's authentic colors which, in the nineteenth century, were subdued by a yellow varnish that blurred the living contrasts and produced an effect of sentimental solemnity.

The subject is taken from the apocryphal Book of Tobit. Tobit, Tobias' father—a second Job, blinded despite a life that was pleasing to God—sent his son to recover a sum of money to provide for his wife after his death. In the course of his journey, the young Tobias, guided by an angel, caught a fish with whose liver he later restored his father's eyesight. Then he recovered the money, found himself a wife, and returned home with her. In the painting she is seen standing in the doorway, praying, next to Hannah, Tobit's wife.

The scene represents the moment when the four characters of the story realize that Tobias' traveling companion who had helped him in his undertaking was an angel of the Lord. The angel, having fulfilled his mission, soars toward heaven in a Michelangelesque posture, his wings glittering with greenish hues. Each of the human figures is affected by this event in a different way. Old Tobit, cured of blindness, is deep in prayer, and his son looks up reverently. Each of the women behind is preoccupied with her own experience, and between them is the frightened dog. This painting does not owe its effect primarily to the colors, as in Rembrandt's later works: the drama of light and dark is here almost more crucial than the colors themselves.

Painted 1638

LANDSCAPE WITH AN OBELISK

Oil on wood, 22 × 28 ¹/₂″

Isabella Stewart Gardner Museum, Boston

It is impossible to form a complete idea of Rembrandt as a landscape painter solely on the basis of the finished and mature examples of his landscapes, such as the one in Cassel, or his etchings dating from the 'forties and the early 'fifties. These later landscapes, bathed in bright sunlight or half-enveloped in shadow, are characterized by breadth of vision and great freedom of composition. Works such as the etching *The Three Trees* (figure 31) give the impression that this is nature, rendered just as we might see it.

The landscapes dating from an earlier period, such as the entire series painted in the late 'thirties, are different in character: they emphasize the drama of nature, the dynamic struggle between elements, the changing sky, the shining forth and the breaking through of sunlight. The landscape in Boston, together with those in Brunswick and Amsterdam, is one of the most important works of this kind. It shows a powerfully orchestrated scene: storm clouds pile up in the distance, pierced by the sun which illuminates the road and the obelisk. It is a great and dramatic vision of nature returning to calm after rain and storm.

The human figures, the rider and his companion, are small, subordinated to the whole. But since the play of colors leads us from the muted background, through the brilliance of the water between two rapids, to the warmth of the foreground with its brightest green in the sunlight—toward which the group is moving—we strongly participate in this experience of the storm and then of the calm which follows. In Rembrandt's paintings even the smallest figures contribute significantly to the mood. We need only recall, for instance, their function in *The Three Trees*.

Painted 1637–50

JOHN THE BAPTIST PREACHING

Oil on canvas, 24 1/2 × 32"

State Museums, Berlin-Dahlem

This grisaille was regarded as a masterpiece even in Rembrandt's lifetime. John, preaching about the future Redeemer, is shown in the brightest light. But many of the surrounding figures take no notice of him: we see children at play, a boy restrained by a maidservant, dogs mating, gypsies sitting impassively, and Pharisees conversing. The spectators include savages and Turks.

This painting which strikes us as so homogeneous in its effect, consists of two parts—the earlier, central section, and the later additions around it. The central section extends up to Caesar's head on the obelisk and cuts through the group of Pharisees below; it is also clearly bounded at the right and left.

This typical chiaroscuro composition of the 'thirties was changed by Rembrandt about 1650 into an entirely new painting. He enlarged the picture and added parts—warmly colored and animated—completely altering the spirit of the earlier composition, and yet one is not conscious of a break in the design. The dark, warm tonality of the later additions acts as a counterpart to the brightness of the center section, but also gives the entire composition the warmth characteristic of Rembrandt's later works. Rembrandt himself was so concerned with this painting—which represents a man who knows what redemption means, preaches about the future Redeemer, and is understood only by a few while life goes on unconcerned—that as late as 1650 he drew two sketches for the frame (see figure 16); to the classical pilasters and cornices he gave a peculiar Baroque animation in keeping with the character of the painting.

Painted 1639

REMBRANDT'S MOTHER

Oil on wood, 32 × 24¹/₂″

Kunsthistorisches Museum, Vienna

Rembrandt's portrait of his mother has been discussed in detail in our Introduction, where we pointed out the emotional effects obtained by means of chiaroscuro and color. We shall note here only the striking contrast between the sparkling jewelry on her bosom and the half-shadowed wrinkled face with its red-rimmed and tired eyes. The woman's posture with both her hands leaning on the stick helps us to understand why many people regard this painting as a symbol of old age rather than as only a portrait of a specific woman, even though this woman is Rembrandt's mother whom he painted so often.

Painted 1639

REMBRANDT'S MOTHER (detail)

Oil on wood

Kunsthistorisches Museum, Vienna

In a book devoted to the lives of Dutch artists published in 1718, the painter-author Arnold Houbraken relates the anecdote that Rembrandt shooed visitors to his studio away from his canvases by saying: "The smell of the paint will annoy you." This remark pertains to Rembrandt's late period, when he applied paint in thick layers with his palette knife, following a technique which deviated completely from that of his contemporaries. Yet with this much earlier painting, too, we feel somehow embarrassed if we examine it, even in reproduction, from very close by. Would Rembrandt have permitted us to get so near to his work?

Once we have overcome our embarrassment, however, we can stand—at least in imagination—face to face with this old woman, Rembrandt's mother, as he painted her in the last year of her life. We do not know precisely how old she was, since her birth date has not been established. In 1589 this baker's daughter, Neeltje Willemsdochter van Zuydhoeck, married the miller Harmen Gerritszoon van Rijn. Rembrandt was the sixth of their seven children. Neeltje survived her husband, who died in 1630, by ten years.

The technique Rembrandt used in this portrait is ideally suited to the dry old skin furrowed with wrinkles. The face is built up with little brush strokes, the lighter parts touched somewhat more heavily than the shaded areas, so that the higher paint catches more light. The tired but still lively eyes, ringed with red, are painted with great love and care. [B.H.]

90

Painted 1642

THE NIGHT WATCH (THE COMPANY OF CAPTAIN FRANS BANNING COCQ)

Oil on canvas, 146 × 175"

Rijksmuseum, Amsterdam

Even though *The Night Watch* is not one of Rembrandt's most completely realized works, this painting, where for the first time he expressed a vast, impetuous, rhythmic movement by means of contrasting colors, was of crucial significance for his development as an artist. Until now he had preferred to merge the separate life of his strong colors in a dark or shadowy space; but here he was compelled to paint broadly and on a big scale. He had been commissioned to paint life-size portraits of Captain Banning Cocq and the members of his Company.

The picture is built entirely on the contrast of colors—yellow and red—which correspond to one another at the right and left of the captain: the little lieutenant with his yellow and blue is counterbalanced by the strange little girl at the left; while the red of the soldiers, the arquebusiers, is distributed on either side, thus emphasizing the movement. But the visual drama of the whole composition derives from the daring use of a non-color, black, in the very center of the composition. This black, bisected by a red sash in the costume of Captain Banning Cocq, is pushed forward by the other colors, and is given a force which could be attained by no previous artist.

The painting as we know it today is mutilated: it was cut when it was moved from its first home in the Kloveniersdoelen in the eighteenth century. Originally it hung fairly high, above a brown wooden wainscoting, where the striking color and light contrasts must have had much more vitality and animation than today, with the picture at the spectator's eye level and under a somewhat contrived lighting.

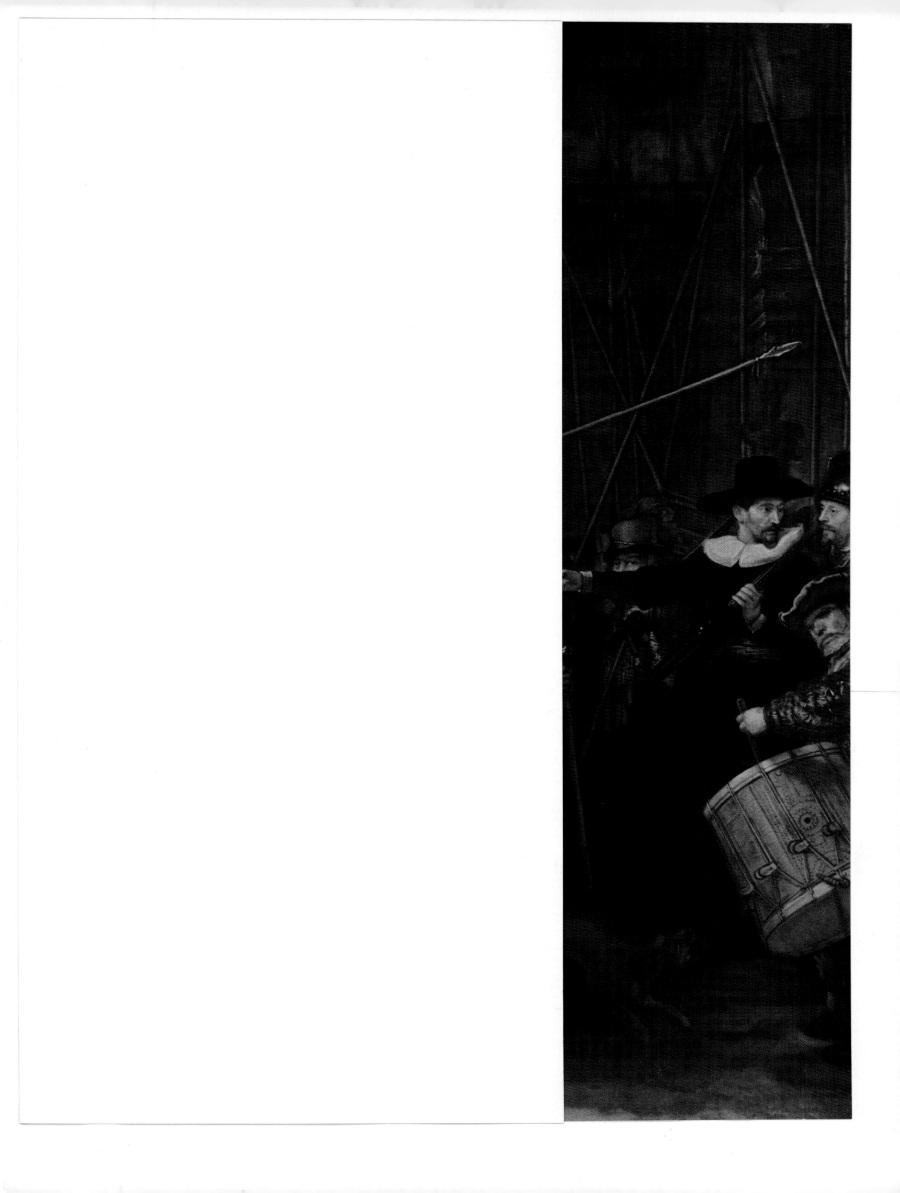

Painted 1642

THE NIGHT WATCH (detail)

Oil on canvas

Rijksmuseum, Amsterdam

As we know, Rembrandt painted the Company of Captain Frans Banning Cocq for the great hall of the arquebusiers—the Kloveniersdoelen—in Amsterdam. The presumed occasion for the commission was the visit to the capital, in 1638, of Marie de' Medici, Queen of France. The great hall contained other civic-guard group portraits, painted in the same period, by such artists as Bartholomeus van der Helst, Govert Flinck, and Joachim von Sandrart. Samuel van Hoogstraten—who might be designated as one of the first Dutch art critics—wrote in 1678 that the painting was so picturesque of concept, so audacious, and so powerful that all the other pieces in the hall looked like so many playing cards. Today three of these large canvases are displayed in the Night Watch Gallery of the Rijksmuseum in Amsterdam, setting off Rembrandt's masterpiece and reinforcing Van Hoogstraten's observation.

The qualities that have made *The Night Watch* famous are easier to discern in this detail than in the reproduction of the whole work. May we draw special attention to the little girl in her remarkable attire, with a chicken and a purse dangling from her belt. Much has been written about this mysterious little figure. What did Rembrandt mean by giving her such prominence in this painting? After all, his commission was to paint the men of Banning Cocq's company as they formed into marching order. If we look at the composition as a whole, we notice immediately that there is an interplay of light between the figures of the lieutenant at right of the captain, and the girl. Irresistibly we are reminded of Manet's answer, two hundred years later, to people who asked him why, in his *Déjeuner sur l'Herbe*, he had painted one woman in the nude, thus bringing a storm of criticism upon himself. He replied: "Because I needed the light effect of nude skin at that point." Might Rembrandt not have given a similar kind of answer if he had been asked why he included the little girl?

Another interesting suggestion has been made by the Dutch art historian Jan Verbeek, who has drawn attention to a painting by Matheus Vroom, *The State Visit of Marie de' Medici to Antwerp*, in the Antwerp Museum. In this painting, too, there is a girl with a chicken tied to her sash; she is in among a group of soldiers and seems to be peddling refreshments to them. Presumably she is a market-girl. If the child in *The Night Watch* is also a market-girl whose presence is accepted quite naturally by the militia, it follows logically that Rembrandt made use of her among the dark figures of the guardsmen to introduce a light effect he needed in his composition. [B.H.]

Painted 1640

THE HOLY FAMILY

Oil on wood, $16^{1}/_{8} \times 13^{3}/_{8}''$
The Louvre, Paris

The subject of the Holy Family, with Joseph as a modest carpenter who must work
to support his family, was treated by Rembrandt several times. One of the most
beautiful versions is this small painting, in which Mary is placed in the brightest
light, with the child reaching out for his mother's breast, while Elizabeth looks up
from her book and glances toward the child.

Rembrandt's intention is clear. He transfers the Biblical scene to his own time,
to the room of a poor carpenter who works contentedly by an open window. A
bright light penetrates from outside, playing on a glass that has been carefully
placed on the sill. Almost entirely in the shadow of the background is a bed, and
by the fireplace sits a cat. It is characteristic of Rembrandt that in this peaceful
scene the Holy Family is treated like an earthly family. And yet it is distinguished
by the lighting which falls on the child and on the floor. Important to our understanding of Rembrandt is the fact that this intimate little painting was created
when he was already working on the tremendous, strictly topical *Night Watch*.

Painted 1644

THE WOMAN TAKEN IN ADULTERY

Oil on wood, 32¹/₂ × 25¹/₂″

National Gallery, London

It would seem that Rembrandt's capacity to produce large paintings was almost exhausted in the 'forties with the completion of *The Night Watch*. Among his subsequent paintings only *The Sacrifice of Manoah*, which is in Dresden (figure 13), is of large size, and even this was probably not completed until about 1650. Rembrandt goes back, one might almost say escapes, to intimate, small-sized paintings; but now these are animated by a new, bright richness of color. Compare, for example, this *Woman Taken in Adultery* with, say, *Simeon in the Temple* dating from 1631, now in The Hague (page 67).

What is decisive here is the way in which the background around the high priest is treated in each of these works. The painting of 1631, for all the concentration of light on the central group, is still largely a matter of darkened and homogeneous space; in the picture opposite we have a far greater differentiation in the glowing light and color. In addition, of course, all resources are used, but in a more lively, more natural way than they were in earlier works. The greater brilliance of the pillars in the background, for instance—so important an element in each composition—is far less conspicuous in its colors than in the *Simeon* of 1631; and yet it is obvious that the steep rise of the pillars above and behind the adulterous woman (just as in the painting of 1631, above Simeon with the child Jesus) is of very great importance for the effect.

As Rembrandt grew older, his themes changed. Whereas in his youth—and again later, in his old age—the concept that men can be redeemed by faith in the coming of the Savior was close to him, in the 'forties he began, with the *Woman Taken in Adultery*, a series of works which mark his preoccupation with man, his sins, and the need for forgiveness. This is the theme of the *Woman Taken in Adultery*, and it perhaps found its most magnificent statement in the drawing of 1659, now in Munich (figure 56).

The painting expresses something entirely different from *The Night Watch*, though the color is used in a similar way. But whereas in *The Night Watch* the whole movement of the picture is a forward rush, here—but still in a different and quieter way than in the *Simeon* of 1631—the effect of the picture is that of a deliberate recession into the middle distance where we see the central figure, the adulterous woman on her knees before Christ. Like Captain Banning Cocq in *The Night Watch*, she is not the figure richest in color; and it is almost because of this lack of color—she is painted in white—that she becomes the center of attention. The colorful circle around her moves back from the red cloak of the man in the turban, passes by the emerald green and blue of the soldier, the guardsman behind the adulterous woman, and leads to the figure which is the climax of the linear structure of the painting—the Christ.

Painted 1648

CHRIST AT EMMAUS

Oil on wood, 27 × 26"

The Louvre, Paris

During the late 'forties Rembrandt painted some of his most mature color compositions, displaying his complete mastery in harmonizing linear and coloristic structure. The diagonal Baroque pattern, the pictorial exuberance, and the pleasure in the sudden and unexpected look of things—all these have given way to a new vision, more simple, more straightforward, but at the same time more deeply stirring. The feeling is now as direct as in devotional paintings, but surpasses them in spirituality.

Christ at Emmaus is a characteristic example of Rembrandt's great compositional skill. Here, the apostles suddenly recognize that the wanderer who has accompanied them to the tavern is the resurrected Lord. Christ, slightly off center, breaks the bread at the brightly lighted table. He is separated, and set off, from his companions by the arch of the lofty niche, almost more than by the bright aura which radiates from him. The painting is entirely built upon the contrasts between very warm colors and the more olive brown and greenish tones of the parts in shadow. When he painted this picture, Rembrandt lived in the Jewish quarter of Amsterdam, and portrayed, among others, the physician Ephraim Bonus (see figure 33); and since he was a careful reader of the Bible, he represented Christ with the face of a Jew.

Rembrandt here gives Christ a more humble, and at the same time more exalted, face than in his earlier representations of the Savior. But when he treated the same subject after 1660—the late and unhappy period of his life—Rembrandt once again returned (as he had in his etching of 1654) to the more conventional conception of Christ as the Lord and Redeemer.

Painted 1648

HANNAH AND SAMUEL

Oil on wood, $15^7/_8 \times 12^1/_2''$

Collection Earl of Ellesmere, London

Another mature and significant work, reflecting Rembrandt's mood of the late 'forties, probably represents the prophetess Hannah and her son Samuel. In the figure of the prophetess with her bright kerchief, the warm purple of the garment, and the little child dressed in olive-green-brown—Rembrandt's son Titus probably served as his model—we already have the full richness of color that was to be the chief characteristic of the later works. But the figures are still largely subordinated to the darkened space. Consider how, from the purely coloristic standpoint, the brilliant gold-yellow, sculptured angel's head above the pews creates color accents and separates the group from the rest of the temple.

In the background at the foot of the tablets of the ten commandments which are ornamented with a brass snake, we can see a kneeling old man holding a child. Rembrandt intended this as a prophetic image of Simeon. Hannah's lending her son to the Lord is a characteristic parallelism in the Old Testament to the story of Simeon in the New Testament.

Painted about 1650

HEAD OF CHRIST

Oil on wood, $9^7/_8 \times 7^7/_8''$
State Museums, Berlin-Dahlem

This head of a young Jew is generally considered to be a study for a figure of Christ. Such an interpretation seems justified when the head is compared with other representations of Christ in Rembrandt's Biblical works (see, for example, *Christ at Emmaus*, page 101). Of a number of similar studies, this panel in Berlin is the best.

There is nothing in the little painting itself to suggest that the head was indeed intended to portray Christ. Nevertheless, on the basis of the assumption that it was, attempts have been made to draw conclusions about Rembrandt's religious convictions. The head presumably resembles most nearly the Mennonite conception of Christ. Yet thoroughgoing research into municipal and church archives has failed to reveal that Rembrandt was ever a member of the Mennonite or any other religious community. He was, however, in close touch with the relatively large group of Mennonites in Amsterdam. When he first arrived there, in 1631, he lodged with the Mennonite art dealer Hendrick van Uylenburgh, and the two men remained friends in later life. Through Van Uylenburgh, Rembrandt received various portrait commissions from wealthy Mennonite burghers. [B.H.]

Painted 1652

AN OLD MAN IN AN ARMCHAIR

Oil on canvas, 44¹/₂ × 35"

The Devonshire Collection, Chatsworth

The 'fifties and the 'sixties bring us Rembrandt's most accomplished portraits. In them he seems quite unconcerned with the patrons who commissioned them. Rather, he uses them as occasions for paintings in which he confronts us with the full range of man's experience and sufferings, displaying his profound understanding of the limits of human nature.

A magnificent example of this art is this old man who supports his shadowed head with his hand. Against a warm brown-green background, absorbed in his thoughts, the old man in his splendid robe sits on a tall brown chair. Decisive for the mood, in connection with the colors of the background, is the way in which our eye is led from the shoulder with its yellow and white, the gold of the doublet, through the tumult of the dark reds which become almost black in the shadow, to the bright colors of the hand which rests on the arm of the chair. The face in half-shadow, with the gray hair and beard, painted in modulated tones, forms an extraordinary, serene climax amidst the turbulent colors of the robes.

Finally, something else—the close-up view—is characteristic of Rembrandt's portraits painted after 1650. Gone is the Baroque arrangement, with its factitious interest; the portraits have a quality of naturalness and immediacy, which is the exact opposite of the fashionable portraits painted by Van Dyck and his school, or by Rembrandt's Dutch contemporaries such as Van der Helst, who supplanted Rembrandt in the favor of the general public.

Painted in 1653

ARISTOTLE CONTEMPLATING THE BUST OF HOMER

Oil on canvas, 54¹/₂ × 52¹/₂"
The Metropolitan Museum of Art, New York

Few of Rembrandt's paintings are so well documented, and few paintings by any artist have been so highly regarded by their owners, as this *Aristotle*. Although the original commission has been lost, we know that Don Antonio Ruffo, a Sicilian nobleman and renowned art collector, must have asked Rembrandt about 1652 to paint the canvas for him. The request is clear proof of Rembrandt's high reputation abroad.

The canvas, dated 1653 by Rembrandt, arrived in 1654 in the harbor of Messina on the Dutch ship "Bartholomeus." The bill of lading, still preserved in the Ruffo family archives, lists the price paid to Rembrandt: five hundred guilders. As Don Antonio himself wrote, that amount was four times as much as he usually paid for a similar painting by the most eminent Italian masters. There is every indication that Don Antonio greatly valued his new acquisition. He gave Rembrandt further commissions and ordered paintings complementary to the *Aristotle* from famous Italian artists. In his will, he bequeathed the best paintings in his collection, including the *Aristotle*, to the eldest Ruffo sons in succession. Sadly enough, in 1743, the eldest son and all his brothers died of the plague, and the Rembrandt passed to another branch of the family, which later sold it. Thereafter it was purchased first by Sir Abraham Hume of England and then by Rodolphe Kann of Paris, two noted collectors. The art dealer Joseph Duveen then took it to the United States where, via the collection of the widow of Collis P. Huntington and that of Alfred W. Erickson, it finally reached the Metropolitan Museum.

The style and grandeur of the *Aristotle* are characteristic of Rembrandt's mature work. The painting is the product of a man at the peak of his powers, master of every technical difficulty, and able to say—with a single stroke and perfect balance—exactly what he wishes to say. A man, too, who has followed his own chosen path, free from the fashions and tastes of his times. About a year after he finished the *Aristotle*, in 1654, he painted the portrait of Jan Six, the most brilliant of his portraits. Rembrandt later surpassed these works only in such paintings as *The Jewish Bride* (page 145). [B.H.]

Painted 1654

BATHSHEBA

Oil on canvas, $56^1/_2 \times 56^1/_2''$
The Louvre, Paris

Bathsheba in this painting is Hendrickje, Rembrandt's faithful helpmate, mistress
and wife, and his companion through his disastrous experiences in the 'fifties. The
picture is essentially a nude, showing, with all of Rembrandt's mastery, the
beautiful body of a woman; but there is scarcely any other work of this kind that
represents, with equal simplicity and greatness, woman, her innocence and her
forlorn condition as a sinner. Bathsheba holds in her hand the letter that will
introduce her to King David. There is something haunting and great in the way in
which everything here expresses beauty and passive submission to fate. The figure
stands out bright against its surroundings—the dark red of the seat, the contrasting
colors of the attendant (in whose coiffure the red glows), and the rich, glittering
cloak behind. The pensive face of this woman with its air of suffering is further
emphasized by the contrast with the resplendent red ornaments of the coiffure.
And how simple, delicate, and forlorn is this hand with which Bathsheba leans on
the white linen!

110

Painted 1654

A WOMAN BATHING

Oil on wood, 24 × 18″
National Gallery, London

This small picture of a woman bathing is not a major work, but it is typical of Rembrandt's ability to transform any passing scene into a work of art. His model here is again Hendrickje; the painting represents a woman cautiously stepping into her bath. She is alone, and unconcernedly lifts her slip, perhaps a little too high. It is an intimate sketch full of contrasts; the figure itself is colorfully brought to life by the rich, loose gown behind her, with its yellows, grays, and reds.

Painted 1655

JOSEPH ACCUSED BY POTIPHAR'S WIFE

Oil on canvas, 44 × 34¹/₂″

State Museums, Berlin-Dahlem

When Hendrickje lived with Rembrandt, in the 'fifties, she served as a model for paintings portraying all the passions of which woman is capable, just as Saskia did in the 'thirties. But while a considerable number of his youthful works depict the evil in women, only one painting dating from the 'fifties represents woman as a seducer. In all other paintings of that period, such as *Bathsheba* and the numerous representations of Christ and the woman of Samaria, woman is portrayed as having preserved her inner purity despite all the sins she must have committed.

The scene showing Joseph accused by Potiphar's wife exists in two versions. One, formerly in Leningrad, now hangs in the National Gallery of Art in Washington; the other is this Berlin picture, which I consider superior. The hand with its fleshy colors that points to Joseph stands out against the white bed, and it is so deliberately placed in the light that it immediately attracts the beholder's attention. Potiphar's lustful wife is dressed in a bright shimmering red which is set off against the deeper red of the chair. All the other colors are subordinated to this main figure, and the color of each figure has its own special character—the garment of the good-natured husband, in brown-olive shot through with yellow; and the deep blue drapery isolating one of the glittering bed posts, which in turn sets off the innocent Joseph despite the dark tones of his garment. If colors can be said to establish the mood of a painting by their polyphony, they surely do so in this work.

Painted 1656

JACOB BLESSING THE SONS OF JOSEPH

Oil on canvas, 68 $\frac{1}{2}$ × 83 $\frac{1}{2}$"

Gemäldegalerie, Cassel

This is one of the few extant large-figured paintings of Rembrandt, in which color serves to render the reality of the scene, while at the same time it directly expresses feelings in all their nuances. The realistic effect is actually achieved by the noble complementary colors surrounding the main group. The powerful red of the bed-cover is, so to speak, complemented by the olive-brown tones of the curtains and the more luminous background.

This is a magnificent representation of the enfeebled patriarch giving his blessing. Supported on his bed, he seems to glow with light amid the bright colors; and the feelings eloquently expressed in all the faces would stir us deeply even if we were unfamiliar with the Biblical text it illustrates. But the significance of this scene will be realized more fully if we recall that Jacob is here represented in his old age, as he blesses Joseph's sons, the older one by his Jewish wife, and the younger by his Egyptian wife Astanath. According to Christian legend, Joseph's younger son symbolizes the future Christian faith. If this is understood, the meaning of Rembrandt's color in this area (see next commentary) becomes clear at once. The almost blind Jacob has unwittingly placed his hand on the head of his younger grandson, while Joseph carefully tries to guide his aged father's hand toward the older boy, who is actually entitled to the blessing. Astanath, the mother of the unjustly chosen boy, is deeply moved and looks on quietly.

116

Painted 1656

JACOB BLESSING THE SONS OF JOSEPH
(detail)

Oil on canvas

Gemäldegalerie, Cassel

In this detail we may see more clearly than ever how Rembrandt can convey through paint the working of the divine will in what appears to be an accident of reality. There is great human understanding in the treatment of Jacob's older, dark-haired grandson who is being slighted. His face looks at us from the shadow, and for all its childishness, it expresses surprise and grief over the unjust humiliation inflicted on him. And how strongly is the light concentrated on the other grandson, who kneels closer to the beholder—on this child who humbly bends his beautiful face, his hands devoutly crossed on his chest, the sign of the Christian cross! Rembrandt, by means of sudden flashes of color in the background, often gives an aura of light to his figures; here too he gives such a seemingly accidental aura of glowing brightness to the face of the younger child.

Painted about 1656

SELF-PORTRAIT

Oil on wood, 20 × 16"

Kunsthistorisches Museum, Vienna

This self-portrait, although small in size, is one of Rembrandt's most important paintings. Rembrandt looks at us frontally, with a serious expression in his steel-blue eyes; he wears his brown working cloak, under which glows the red jerkin. This red is reflected in the dignified face of a man who, at precisely this time, was passing through one of the severest ordeals of his life.

It is perhaps the last of the series of Rembrandt's self-portraits to show him as a man full of vigor; he looks at us sternly, inquiring, and yet full of kindness. The head is still framed in dark, reddish-brown locks. A year later they were to turn color, for, beginning with the self-portraits of 1657 and 1658 (the year of the auction of Rembrandt's possessions), his face is framed in gray locks, even though his moustache remained blond for a long time. The self-portraits dating from the last decade of his life show him as a prematurely aged man. But while his features mirror all of life's sufferings, they also show a determination to meet them with dignity. These later works today move us almost more than those dating from his youth and successful manhood.

Painted about 1656

TWO YOUNG NEGROES

Oil on canvas, 30¹/₂ × 25"
Mauritshuis, The Hague

Rembrandt rarely portrayed people as merely the representatives of authority, and even where he did so, as in *The Night Watch*, he was more interested in catching their individual traits—for instance, the vanity of Captain Banning Cocq and the subservience of his lieutenant. In Rembrandt's late work this urge to paint people becomes so powerful as to defy all conventions.

Negroes have often been portrayed by European painters since the Renaissance (one of the three Magi is a Moorish king); they were usually treated with naturalistic accuracy, but with a sense of aloofness, so that their individual character was not fully grasped. Rembrandt's picture displays no such attitude of superiority; he portrays his Negroes with humanity and understanding. The dark pigments used here to render the black faces stand out so vividly only because the background is painted in subdued olive tones. Rembrandt's other paintings of this period generally show a richer and purer color orchestration.

Painted about 1657

THE POLISH RIDER

Oil on canvas, 46 × 53"
The Frick Collection, New York

This relatively small equestrian portrait once again reveals something entirely new: it can scarcely be called a portrait, for the figure blends with landscape so that the two are completely unified. The rider does not move toward us as he does in Rembrandt's other extant equestrian portrait, that of Frederick Rihel (page 143). This horseman, his head turned toward us, moves across the painting. The force of the movement, the play of colors, and above all the new dynamic arrangement of lights and darks, are extraordinary. The rider, his garment, and the rump of his horse—which has the vitality of the horses in the great Parthenon sculptures—are bathed in a mysterious light, while the horse's head is in shadow. It is understandable that modern beholders should attach special symbolic significance to this rider irresistibly moving across the landscape, and that he should remind them of Dürer's knight in the etching, *Knight, Death, and the Devil.*

Painted about 1657–58

A BOY READING (TITUS)

Oil on canvas, 28 × 24³/₈″

Kunsthistorisches Museum, Vienna

This is a portrait of Rembrandt's son Titus, who in this period often appears in his paintings and drawings. It exemplifies the mature Rembrandt's dynamic style, his simultaneous use of thick impasto and glazes, as well as his power to express human life in its passing moods. The painting portrays the withdrawn quality of a young man absorbed in his reading. Harmony—and in Rembrandt harmony always means balanced tension and contrast—arises here from the interplay and opposition of the brightest colors, such as the strands of yellow and red in the locks, the reddish hand, the bit of yellow glowing in the bookcover, and the rich dark tones in the background and in the garment.

Painted 1659

MOSES BREAKING THE TABLETS OF THE LAW

Oil on canvas, 66¹/₂ × 54"

State Museums, Berlin-Dahlem

Even though this may be only a fragment of a larger painting, it is certain that Rembrandt himself cut it out of the original composition after it had been refused by those who commissioned it.

The glow of the yellow letters on the dark tablets is part of a moving interplay of light and colors. This interplay is continued in the brightly lit sleeves, contrasting with the half-shadow from which the head emerges. It is the profoundly expressive face of a man who had set out to bring happiness and order, but on his return sees how men really are. Moses is painted with great breadth; the figure is designed for long-range effect. The small reproduction can give only a remote idea of its impact.

Painted 1660

ST. PETER DENYING HIS MASTER

Oil on canvas, 61 × 67"

Rijksmuseum, Amsterdam

The period of Rembrandt's trials suggested to him a new subject—that of a basically good man who, for fear of his life, is ready to disavow and betray everything he has lived for. Betrayal, surrender, and all the torments these imply are portrayed in this painting.

It shows Peter being asked by a servant whether he is a follower of Christ, who is seen in the background before the high priest. Peter's face is illuminated by the servant's candle. The scene in the foreground, for all its magnificence, is hauntingly realistic; there is a soldier whose coarse features brand him as an evil-doer, and whose helmet resting on his knees gleams in the light. The Negro soldier behind him looks at Peter without comprehending the meaning of the scene. Peter's face expresses infinite grief; it is partly in the shadow, because the brightest light is on his shoulder and around the candle held by the servant, who shades it with her hand. Behind Peter, at the right, we see Christ, livid, half-dark. As He had prophesied, Peter was to deny Him before the cock had crowed thrice.

The color in this picture conveys the interplay of contrasting realms of feeling. The foreground, with its powerful, earthy colors, is in opposition to the muted tonality of the background scene with Christ. Between the two zones are the strongest, the most dynamic colors, ranging from the brightest red and yellow to the more subdued shades of Peter's garment.

130

Painted about 1660

JACOB WRESTLING WITH THE ANGEL

Oil on canvas, 54 × 45⁵/₈"

State Museums, Berlin-Dahlem

Genesis 32 : 22–32 relates that Jacob, having sent his family and possessions across the brook Jabbok, spent the whole of one night wrestling with a stranger who, unable to defeat him, "touched the hollow of his thigh; and the hollow of Jacob's thigh was out of joint." When dawn broke, the antagonist was revealed to be an angel of the Lord. In painting the episode, Rembrandt depicts the moment at which the angel dislocates Jacob's hip.

The original canvas was definitely larger than the present state. The signature, probably inscribed on a piece of the canvas that was cut off, now appears in the lower right corner. In style and composition the painting strongly resembles *Moses Breaking the Tablets of the Law* (page 129). The figures in both paintings are built up of large color areas placed against indefinable backgrounds. The face of the angel is especially noteworthy here; it shows no trace of physical exertion but only compassion for Jacob. [B.H.]

Painted about 1661

MATTHEW THE EVANGELIST

Oil on canvas, 37³/₄ × 31⁷/₈″

The Louvre, Paris

About 1661 Rembrandt painted a number of apostles and evangelists. All these paintings are more or less the same size, and all portray half-figures. Nothing is known of a commission, and it is tempting to regard this impressive series of men's figures as a completely independent venture by the artist—a trial of his own power to depict in ordinary human faces the individual character of the men who accompanied or wrote about Jesus.

The *Self-Portrait as the Apostle Paul*, in the Rijksmuseum at Amsterdam, and *Matthew the Evangelist* are perhaps the most fascinating portraits in the series. As Matthew sits writing his Gospel in a large folio volume, he listens to the heavenly inspiration that comes from an angel whispering over his shoulder. His face is magnificent in its tense concentration as he tries to catch the angel's words. [B.H.]

134

Painted 1661

THE CIRCUMCISION

Oil on canvas, 22¹/₂ × 30″

The National Gallery of Art, Washington, D.C. (Widener Collection)

Rembrandt made many versions of the circumcision of Christ. Here it is treated in a unique way: instead of the usual scene with the child in the priest's lap and Mary a mere spectator, we have a tribute to Mary, mother of the Redeemer, for it is she who holds the child. The main group is arranged with quiet simplicity in a classical triangular composition; the scribes look at the group, and among them a man in the extreme left background has Rembrandt's own features.

Painted 1662

THE SYNDICS (THE SAMPLING OFFICIALS OF THE DRAPERS' GUILD)

Oil on canvas, 74 × 109¹/₂"

Rijksmuseum, Amsterdam

This painting represents a meeting of the Board of the Drapers' Guild. As a group portrait it goes far beyond the many group portraits of regents of humanitarian organizations that were so characteristic of Holland. The beholder who stands in front of this painting—it should hang fairly high—is seized with respect before these men who look at him directly with a questioning yet kindly expression; they are obviously concerned, because one of them has even risen from his seat.

Rembrandt's ability to define our relationship to the picture by means of color is here triumphantly apparent. The red of the carpet, this powerful color, places these men above us and sets them off as judges and helpers, while at the same time an inner cohesion is achieved through the closely related tones of the background and the black of the garments. Those able to grasp the pattern of lines and the rhythm of a composition need not be told by what means the beholder's glance is directed so unfailingly to the chairman, a small man who sits in the center, accentuated through the taller regent to the left of him and the standing servant in the background. The warm light that falls on all the figures is a link between them and us, and since they look at us directly we cannot elude their spell.

Painted 1662

THE CONSPIRACY OF THE BATAVIANS

Oil on canvas, 78 × 123¹/₂"

Nationalmuseum, Stockholm

This work is only a fragment. Rembrandt was commissioned to paint the subject—the sketches for it have survived—as a decoration for one of the walls of the new Town Hall in Amsterdam. But it seems that his radical, aggressive color scheme and his novel approach found less favor than the conventional and not very interesting decorative works of his pupils, Flinck and Ovens, which have been preserved to this day.

The subject of this painting pertains to Dutch history. The Batavians are the ancestors of the Dutch, and their revolt under Claudius Civilis against the Romans in the first century would have evoked in Rembrandt's contemporaries patriotic feelings and memories of the recent struggle against Spain.

It seems likely that Rembrandt himself later cut up the painting, preserving only the central part, which represents the Batavian chief to whom his followers swear that they will take revenge on the Romans. The color scheme is full of vigor, extremely alive and warm. These colors lead us in the direction of the one-eyed ruler, who stands out against the reds and dark blues with his tall blue cap and his yellow jerkin. He holds a sword upon which they take the oath that they will stand together against their powerful enemy.

Painted 1663?

EQUESTRIAN PORTRAIT

Oil on canvas, 113 × 94"

National Gallery, London

The great sensation of the exhibition of Dutch art in London, 1953, was the portrait of a horseman which, although known in reproduction, had not been publicly exhibited in recent times. It probably represents Frederick Rihel, in whose will it is recorded in 1681. Whatever academicians may find objectionable in this work—for instance, the way the horse is painted—it exemplifies the new power of Rembrandt's colors. There is some dispute as to whether the picture should be dated 1649 or 1663, but it is undeniable that the impact of this rider in his yellow coat is tremendous.

Light and dark are here completely transformed into a harmonious play of colors. In order to experience this picture fully we must be aware of the autumnal red woods with the curious coach and the gray-blue sky. European art since the Renaissance has produced a number of important equestrian portraits; this is one of the masterpieces in this field, equal to Titian's *Charles V at the Battle of Mühlberg* and the equestrian portraits of Velázquez.

Painted about 1668

THE BRIDAL COUPLE
(THE JEWISH BRIDE)

Oil on canvas, 47 × 65 ¹/₂″

Rijksmuseum, Amsterdam

In the last years of his life Rembrandt created two great masterpieces, one of which is this so-called *Jewish Bride*. With a sketchy landscape as its background, it is a pageant of colors and vivid contrasts painted with a mastery that has become entirely free. Scholars have established that this type of portrait goes back to Italian Renaissance scenes of marriage or betrothal.

The red of the woman's garment is complemented by the greenish undertones in the dress of the man, and by the brightness of the yellow impasto on his arm. Whether the alternate title *Jewish Bride* is correct, or whether the painting actually shows Rembrandt's son (who was soon to die of consumption) and his bride, can no longer be determined. But the coloristic power and the tenderness of the two lovers still retain their original impact.

Painted about 1668–69

A MARRIED COUPLE
WITH THREE CHILDREN

Oil on canvas, 50 × 66¹/₂″

Herzog Anton-Ulrich Museum, Brunswick

It is generally assumed that this family scene was painted even later than *The Jewish Bride*. Here, more powerfully perhaps than in any other work of Rembrandt's, the element of portraiture is raised to the level of symbolism. This mother with her child is like the Madonna with the infant Jesus in certain Renaissance paintings where she is shown receiving the tribute of saints or donors. The structure of the color is extremely concentrated. At the left, the composition culminates in the husband, who tenderly leads the older children with their basket of flowers to the wife with the youngest child. The colors of this group, with their variety of green tones, find a complement in the carmines and scarlets of the mother and child at the right. This painting has recently been restored. What we have said about it here is based on notes taken years before the last restoration.

146

Painted about 1668–69 (?)

THE RETURN OF THE PRODIGAL SON

Oil on canvas, $103^{1}/_{8} \times 80^{3}/_{4}''$

The Hermitage, Leningrad

Love is the theme of two of Rembrandt's last large canvases: *The Jewish Bride*, portraying the love between man and woman, and *The Return of the Prodigal Son*, depicting a father's forgiving love for an errant child. In both paintings the essence of love seems concentrated in the hands. In *The Jewish Bride*, the man's hand is placed on the woman's breast and is touched by her fingertips in a gesture of infinite tenderness. The father's hands in the *Prodigal Son* clasp the threadbare shoulders of the son, who has fallen abjectly to his knees. As the old man draws to his breast the son he thought lost, his grief is transformed into deep gratitude.

Rembrandt had treated the return of the prodigal son many times in his drawings and etchings. If we compare these earlier works with this painting, we realize the enormous psychological and artistic distance he had covered. Whereas he had formerly sought dramatic effect through movement, he here achieves a far more powerful impact through the subdued intensity of these figures. Like the son, the viewer is caught in the father's benedictory embrace.

The onlookers in the painting, the figures at the right, contribute little emotionally or pictorially to the composition. They are so inferior in quality that it is difficult to imagine that Rembrandt painted them. The most acceptable explanation would seem to be that Rembrandt never got beyond sketching these figures and that the painting was completed by someone else. This conclusion is borne out by the signature—*R V Ryn f.*—never otherwise used by Rembrandt. [B.H.]

148

Painted 1669

SELF-PORTRAIT

Oil on canvas, 23 ^{1}/$_2$ × 20"
Mauritshuis, The Hague

It is difficult to say why we are so deeply moved by Rembrandt's last self-portrait, painted at a time when all those he loved were gone. Hendrickje had died in 1663, and his son Titus, if he was still alive, was married and separated from his father. It is the portrait of a lonely man who examines himself, his inner life, so to speak, and the marks which suffering have inflicted upon his features. And yet, although the colors are subdued—what a long way from the first youthful self-portrait to this one!—it is a painting that hauntingly expresses genuine humanity. For here, Rembrandt is once more determined to look at himself, even though the eyes that saw so much look tired, and the mouth is sorrowful.

This aged man with white hair does not give up the struggle. The splendor of life on this earth is still amazingly felt in these features. The background is painted in subdued colors reminiscent of those in Rembrandt's youthful works. The figure is nevertheless clearly set off against it. But while in the early works life is rendered by the brightness of the colors, and while the works dating from the early 'sixties are distinguished by their full, sumptuous tones, here the subdued tonality of the whole expresses fulfillment and serenity. This is an autumnal mood—the end of the road: the colors sparkle and glimmer in the cap, as a counterpoint to the white locks and the dark eyes.